FOREVER AMBER

FROM NOVEL TO FILM

D1596249

FOREVER AMBER

FROM NOVEL TO FILM

GARY A. SMITH

Published in the USA by:
BearManor Media
PO Box 1129
Duncan, Oklahoma 73534-1129
www.bearmanormedia.com

ISBN 978-1-59393-543-6

Printed in the United States of America
Book design by Brian Pearce | Red Jacket Press

TABLE OF CONTENTS

Dedicated to George Meyers in appreciation of his encouragement and enthusiasm for this project.

ACKNOWLEDGEMENTS

I WOULD LIKE TO THANK THE FOLLOWING INDIVIDUALS AND institutions for their help and/or encouragement in writing this book: Michael Hirschbein, Marty Kearns, Rudy Behlmer, Karl Thiede, Robert Reynolds, John Rechy, 20th Century-Fox, Larry Edmunds' Bookstore, Ned Comstock at the U.S.C. Doheny Library of Cinema and Television, Julie Graham at the U.C.L.A. Library Special Collections, Barbara Hall at the Academy of Motion Picture Arts and Sciences Library, the American Film Institute Library, Alysoun Sanders at Macmillan Publishers U.K., Linda Ho Peche of the Harry Ransom Humanities Research Center at The University of Texas at Austin, Ben Alexander at the New York Public Library, Jonathan Hahn at the Chicago Preview Press, and Howard Mandlebaum at Photofest.

Some of the information in this book was also taken from personal correspondence with Vincent Price, John Russell, David Raksin, and Philip Dunne in April 1987, Kathleen Winsor in June 1988, and Peggy Cummins-Dunnett in January 1995.

INTRODUCTION

A MAMMOTH HISTORICAL ROMANCE WRITTEN BY A FIRST-TIME female author is published by Macmillan Company. The book becomes a tremendous bestseller. The movie rights are optioned by a powerful Hollywood producer who conducts a talent hunt for an actress to play the part of the tempestuous heroine of the novel. Numerous scripts are written, directors come and go and, after much tribulation, the finished film is a box-office hit. You might think I am referring to *Gone with the Wind*, but you would be wrong. Although all of the above statements are true of Margaret Mitchell's classic Civil War story, they are also true of the now far lesser-known *Forever Amber*.

"Why *Forever Amber*?" you may ask…and rightly so. The easiest answer would be to say that it is one of my favorite books and also one of my favorite movies. But my reasons for writing this book run deeper than that. *Forever Amber* was the best-selling novel of the forties and the film version was one of the most eagerly anticipated of its day, rivaling *Gone with the Wind* for public interest. The title became a household word and today is still remembered by just about anybody who was around during that period. "Ah, yes…*Forever Amber*, it was quite a dirty book at the time," is the usual response. However, in recent years it has slipped into relative obscurity. Although the novel has seldom, if ever, been out of print since it was first published in 1944, few people seem to be familiar with it now. The film version has faired only slightly better because of occasional showings on television.

The fame of *Forever Amber* was based on its notoriety. The book deals frankly with a period of history which was infamous for its excesses, both sexual and otherwise. This explicit approach upset critics and clergy who widely condemned the novel. Hoping to repress the book, instead they accomplished the reverse and stimulated public interest. When a film version was announced, the voices of morality once again moved into high gear and attempted to prevent its production. The controversy which surrounded *Forever Amber* may have sold tremendous amounts of books and cinema tickets, but it also prevented both the novel and the motion picture from being taken seriously on their own merits. The title simply could not escape its reputation. The journey of *Forever Amber* from novel to film is, in part, a story of censorship and the damaging effect it can have on the creative process, be it writing or filmmaking.

With the death of *Forever Amber* author Kathleen Winsor in 2003, many of her eulogizers reevaluated the novel and praised the historical detail which she had so painstakingly written into it. A reevaluation of the film version is also needed and long overdue. Although a marvel of its time from a technical standpoint, the movie was all but ignored by the Academy of Motion Picture Arts and Sciences. It received a single nomination (for Best Original Score) with no acknowledgment given to the extraordinary cinematography, costumes, and production design. One cannot help but wonder if this would have been the case if the reputation of the film had not been so notorious.

I feel that one of the major reasons for the descent of *Forever Amber* into obscurity is that it is no longer considered controversial. What was a "dirty book" and a "scandalous" motion picture in the forties, seems incredibly tame by today's moral standards. But now is the time to look at both the movie and the novel for what they are and not what they were once perceived to be.

CHAPTER ONE

Kathleen Winsor

who, at age twenty-five, was to become one of the most famous authors of her time. Kathleen was born to Harold and Myrtle Winsor on October 16, 1919, in Olivia, Minnesota. Harold was a real estate salesman who moved his wife and their two children to California when Kathleen was still a child. Later, as a student at the University of California at Berkeley, she met Robert J. Herwig, who was a center on the all-American football team there. They married in 1936 while both were still in college. When her husband was doing his senior thesis on Charles II, Kathleen read one of his source books and became interested in the Restoration period of England.

Kathleen graduated college in 1938 and took a job as a receptionist at the *Oakland Tribune* newspaper. Eventually becoming a reporter, she contributed a series of articles to the paper which examined football from a woman's perspective. During this time Kathleen also continued to extensively research the Restoration. She read over 350 books on the subject and filled four notebooks with information and detailed water-color sketches of that period of English history. Determined to write a bestseller, she began working on a novel in February 1940. The story, set in England during the reign of Charles II, relates the tribulations and love affairs of the beautiful Amber St. Clare as she climbs the social ladder from country wench to the lofty position of the King's Mistress.

In 1941 America entered World War II and, shortly thereafter, Robert Herwig began a tour of duty with the Marines. Kathleen used the solitude to finish her book, which she dedicated to "Lieutenant Robert John Herwig, U.S.M.C.R." After five years of research and writing, which included six drafts of the manuscript, Kathleen sent the completed novel, entitled *Wings of the Morning*, to The Macmillan Company in New York City. The manuscript was over 2,500 pages in length and no carbon copy had been made by the author. She mailed it in a wooden butcher box that had originally contained a ham.

In 1936 Macmillan had scored a huge success with first-time author Margaret Mitchell whose Civil War romance, *Gone with the Wind*, became one of the biggest bestsellers of all time. Harold Latham, who had discovered Mitchell, was the Vice President of Macmillan when the manuscript of *Wings of the Morning* was submitted to them. In his autobiography, *My Life in Publishing*, Latham expresses his definite lack of enthusiasm for the novel. After reading the manuscript, he decided that it did not fit the "pure and above reproach" Macmillan standards and cast his vote against accepting it. He did not feel it belonged in the catalogue of a publisher with "important educational and religious departments." The sales manager, convinced it had tremendous sales potential, fought this decision and eventually won out. Macmillan gave Kathleen a $50,000 advance for the rights to publish her work. She was brought from California to assist the editors in cutting it down to a more acceptable length and to revise some of the passages which were considered too salacious by the powers that be at Macmillan. Years later Kathleen said, "I wrote only two sexy passages, and my publishers took both of them out. They put in ellipses instead. In those days, you could solve everything with an ellipse." Macmillan was also not happy with the original title, *Wings of the Morning*. Prior to publication, an exasperated staff member was discussing the novel in a meeting and said, "I get a little tired of Amber — it's forever Amber, forever Amber" and from that chance remark the final title was derived.

Forever Amber was published on October 16, 1944, which was Kathleen Winsor's 25th birthday. The book was an instant sensation. In the first week of release there were over 100,000 copies sold and within a month the novel went into a second printing. *Forever Amber* was on the *New York Times* bestseller list for seventy-five weeks. So great was the demand for copies that Macmillan ran the following statement in the November 11, 1944, issue of *Publisher's Weekly*: "We can't accept any further orders for delivery this year. The copies which will be available between now and Christmas are being rationed among orders already on hand. We suggest that you place your firm order now for delivery in the new year."

The same day that *Forever Amber* went on sale, Kathleen Winsor embarked on a national book tour. Her first stop was the Boston Book Fair. Ironically, three days later, the book was banned in Massachusetts as obscene. Attorney General George Rowell upheld the request by stating that the novel had "70 references to sexual intercourse; 30 illegitimate pregnancies; 7 abortions; 10 descriptions of women dressing, undressing, or bathing in the presence of gentle-men; 5 references to incest; 13 references ridiculing marriage; and 49 miscellaneous objectionable passages." The novel was censored in fourteen other states as well.

America wasn't the only country where *Forever Amber* encountered censorship problems. The Australian Literature Censorship Board banned the novel outright. Senator Keane, the Australian Minister for Customs, said at the time, "I consider it an undesirable book and not an acquisition to the literature of the Commonwealth. The Almighty did not give people eyes to read that rubbish." Dr. L.H. Allen, chair of the Literature Censorship Board, remarked, "Popularity is no sure guarantee of worth" and declared that the book "merely stimulates salacious interest." The ban in Australia on *Forever Amber* would not be lifted until 1958.

Of course, all of this controversy merely fueled the public's curiosity and within a year it was into its eleventh printing. Apparently even the President of the United States wasn't immune to Amber's allure. During the War years, Franklin Roosevelt read "light novels" for relaxation. In Joseph E. Persico's book *Roosevelt's Secret War*, the author says: "When an aide asked if [Roosevelt] had read Kathleen Winsor's racy best-seller…he answered with a twinkle in his eye, 'Only the dirty parts.'"

The charm and beauty of author Kathleen Winsor also contributed to the novel's success. Although Harold Latham may not have cared for her book, he later said that "Kathleen Winsor as a personality was a publisher's dream. She was a perfect illustration of the invaluable help that an author can be in public relations." Latham stated that a rival publisher once remarked that "half the success of *Forever Amber* was due to the bewitching charm of its creator and to the skill with which the publisher capitalized on her presence." Macmillan spent $20,000 to publicize the novel and the comely, first-time author was a key factor in their promotion. But writer Taylor Caldwell, who thought Kathleen was "one of America's most magnificent novelists," lamented that her good looks worked against her ever being taken seriously as an author.

The public may have loved Kathleen Winsor's brainchild, but critical consensus was generally not kind. Most literary critics chose to ignore the vast amount of historical research that had gone into the novel and, instead, concentrated on the sexual exploits of its high-spirited and immoral heroine. *Catholic World* declared that "bawdy incidents are ground out relentlessly without humor or variety." *Saturday Review* said that "the book is incredibly vulgar, no fare for squeamish souls." *Yale Review* called it "a crude and superficial glorification of a courtesan." Some of the critics who chose to look beyond the controversial aspects of the novel, found merit in Kathleen Winsor's writing. *The Chicago Sunday Tribune* stated that "the writing is quick, often witty, seldom obtrusive." *Harper's* found it "a real achievement in characterization and romantic storytelling." *New York Times Book Review* called the author "a born storyteller," but such critical praise for the novel was definitely in the minority.

While Kathleen was enjoying her newly acquired fame on the home front, her husband Robert had achieved another kind of recognition in the South Pacific. In a July 18, 1945, *Time* article, entitled "Forever Herwig," it was reported that Lieut. Robert J. Herwig had distinguished himself for bravery on several occasions as a platoon leader of the 6th Marine Division, thereby winning the Navy Cross for "extraordinary heroism." Unfortunately, the article ends on a demeaning note by saying his greatest claim to fame is that he is the husband of the author of the "sex-best-seller" *Forever Amber*. In Europe, a B-24 Liberator Bomber aircraft of the 718th Squadron was christened "Forever Amber," complete with "nose art" depicting a buxom babe. While Amber's namesake flew the skies over postwar Europe, the novel was finally released in England in September 1945. It had been delayed due to a wartime paper shortage. *Time* declared that "English critics thumbed through and condemned it as tedious, bad writing, and worse taste." The book reviewer for the September 24, 1945, edition of Britain's *Evening Standard* said: "Miss Winsor has attempted an erotic novel on a grand scale, swoony with ill-defined sex, written in a style that rasps the nerves like a Brooklyn accent. I gave up on page 272, by which time Amber had reached her eighth man." But, as in the United States, bad reviews did not keep the public from snapping it up in droves. By the end of 1945, *Forever Amber* had sold 897,366 copies in America. The book went on to become the best-selling U.S. novel of the 1940s, eventually selling over three million copies worldwide.

The instantaneous and overwhelming success of *Forever Amber* gave Kathleen Winsor the bestseller she had been seeking, but wealth and notoriety didn't seem to bring her happiness. After her husband got out of the service, the couple purchased an expensive home in the West-wood area of Los Angeles about a mile from where her novel was being turned into a motion picture. But Robert Herwig was unable to cope with his wife's sudden success and she was unwilling to return to the role of a housewife. In 1946, their marriage ended in divorce and the novel's original dedication is absent from later editions of the book. She married three more times, most infamously to bandleader Artie Shaw from 1946 to 1948. After 21 months Kathleen filed for divorce. Her divorce petition claimed that Shaw was "drunk, abusive, and belligerent" and that he had "screamed at her and beaten her." The tabloids had a field day with all of this. In 1949 she married Arnold Krawkower, a lawyer whom she would eventually divorce in 1953.

Kathleen's next novel, *Star Money*, came out in 1950. It tells the story of a successful first-time author who writes a controversial book which brings her fame and fortune but not happiness. In this thinly-veiled auto-biographical novel, the main character, Shireen Delaney, says, "It's funny, but I guess I must have expected that if I got my book published and made a lot of money, everything would be solved. And nothing is, after all. I'm still no happier than I was before - maybe not even as happy as when I was working, because then I at least had a lot of illusions that I don't have now."

While Kathleen was married to Arnold Krawkower, he pointed out to her that she had paid too much in taxes on the money she received when she sold the movie rights to *Forever Amber*. He informed her that she should have paid only a 25% capital gains tax rather than regular income tax. In 1951 Kathleen filed action in the U.S. Court of Claims to recover part of the taxes she had paid and *Forever Amber* was a news item once again. A hearing was held on June 28, 1951, and, nearly a year later, on June 3, 1952, she was awarded a $52,717 tax refund. That same year her next book, *The Lovers*, was published.

In 1956, Kathleen met and married her last husband, lawyer Paul Porter, a former head of the U.S. Federal Communications Commission. The following year she published *America with Love*, which garnered some of the best reviews of her entire career. For the better part of the next two decades she was a Washington, D.C., society hostess who rarely alluding to her former celebrity, although she continued to work on another massive historical novel during this time. After seven years of research and writing, in 1965, *Wanderers Eastward, Wanderers West* was published. This would become Kathleen Winsor's second most successful book. The story is set in America during the 19th Century and again shows her incredible flare for period detail. *Time* called it "A remarkable novel" and *Saturday Review* said, "Miss Winsor has a wonderful ability to delineate character, to make people come alive, seem real." When Paul Porter died in 1975, Kathleen moved back to New York City where she continued her writing career with *Calais* (1979) and *Jacintha* (1985). Her final novel, *Robert and Arabella*, was published in 1986.

Kathleen Winsor spent her last years as a recluse in her Upper East Side home, mostly forgotten by the public that had once given her such widespread adoration and fame. She died there at age 83 on May 26, 2003. Although she wrote seven novels after *Forever Amber*, none of them ever approached the success of her first. A sequel, *Amber in America*, was often mentioned but never written. In 2002 a new edition of *Forever Amber* was published with a foreword by Barbara Taylor Bradshaw, who acknowledged the debt owed Kathleen Winsor by all romance novelists and called the novel "a genuine page turner...a smashing read." In *Twentieth-Century Romance and Historical Writers*, Christian H. Moe says that "Forever Amber, with its brazen central character and vivid historicity, stands as a significant achievement which influenced the shaping of the contemporary romance novel as a genre." Eric Homberger, in his obituary of Kathleen Winsor in *The Guardian*, less eloquently called her the "author who launched the bodice ripper boom."

The most heartfelt article to appear after her death was written by author John Rechy for the *Los Angeles Times Book Review*. He ended it by saying: "Posterity has a way of correcting literary misjudgment, eventually relegating to derisive footnotes fatuous censorious attorneys general, clownish judges, silly reviewers, uninformed obituary writers. The frail lady who died on May 26 was the woman who created Amber St. Clare. Amber survived plague and fire. With equal assurance, her creator triumphs."

Surely, no author could hope for a finer epitaph.

CHAPTER TWO
The Novel

A NOVEL AS COMPLEX AS *FOREVER AMBER* MUST BE READ IN ITS entirety to be fully appreciated. No brief synopsis can ever do justice to the period detail and historical facts that are presented in great abundance. But, it would be difficult to proceed with any discussion of the film without some knowledge of the story. In this synopsis, the historical subplots involving Charles II and the various court intrigues are, for the most part, not included.

It is worth pointing out that Amber's surname is spelled three different ways within the Prologue and first two chapters: St. Claire, St. Clare, and St. Clair. Throughout the remainder of the novel it is always St. Clare. This occurs in every edition of the book I have seen.

PROLOGUE — 1644

Judith Marsh, daughter of Lord William Marsh, is betrothed to John Mainwaring, son of the Earl of Rosswood. Their marriage is about to take place when Civil War breaks out in England between the Royalists, who support King Charles I, and the Parliamentarians led by Oliver Cromwell. Judith's family is ardent Royalists and John's have joined the Parliamentarian cause. This creates a feud between the two families and the wedding is called off.

Despite the protests of her parents, Judith continues to love John, who has gone off to fight in the war. In an effort to make her forget him, Lord Marsh arranges for his daughter to marry Edmund Mortimer, Earl of Radclyffe, whom she loathes on sight. When John contrives to meet with Judith, they make love and vow to marry despite their parents' objections. Shortly thereafter, Judith discovers she is pregnant.

As the Parliamentary forces are about to descend on the Marsh estate, John returns and offers to take Judith and her mother to safety. Lady Marsh refuses, but Judith goes with him to a farmhouse in the village of Marygreen where he presents her as his wife, Judith St. Claire. The farmer, Matthew Goodegroome, and his wife Sarah welcome Judith into their family. When Judith dies in childbirth and John fails to return from the war, Matthew and Sarah adopt the orphaned baby, who had been named Amber by her dying mother.

PART ONE

On May 5, 1660, a band of Cavaliers, led by Lord Bruce Carlton, rides into the rural village of Marygreen on their way to London. They have come from abroad with the news that King Charles II will soon arrive in England to reclaim his throne. Amber St. Clare, sixteen years old and already a great beauty, contrives to meet Lord Carlton and falls madly in love with him. He responds by making love to her after which she convinces him to take her to London. They are accompanied by his good friend and fellow Cavalier John Randolph, Earl of Almsbury.

Bruce and Amber take lodgings at the Royal Saracen in London and, on May 29, King Charles II returns to the city, heralding the beginning of the Restoration. One day while Bruce is out on business, Almsbury attempts to make love to Amber but she refuses, explaining that it is Bruce she loves. Meanwhile, Bruce is attempting to get financing from the King to buy ships for a privateering venture. Shortly after the King approves of Bruce's plan, Amber realizes that she is pregnant. Despite her situation, Bruce sails off, leaving her a five-hundred-pound recompense.

Alone in London, Amber is befriended by Sally Goodman, an older woman who is also residing at the Royal Saracen. Sally introduces Amber to her nephew, Luke Channel, who seems quite taken with his aunt's new friend. Although she is fairly repulsed by him, Amber agrees to marry Luke because she does not want to endure the stigma of being an unwed mother. The marriage turns out to be a plot by Sally and Luke to swindle Amber out of her money. They leave her penniless and owing a three-hundred-ninety-seven-pound debt.

PART TWO

Amber has been sentenced to the Lady Debtor's Ward in Newgate Prison. She becomes friends with a slattern named Moll Turner who explains that in order to survive, Amber must give bribes to the jailer's wife, Mrs. Cleggat. While in prison, Amber catches the eye of Black Jack Mallard, a notorious highwayman, who offers his protection if she will become his mistress. When Black Jack escapes, he takes Amber with him to a thieves' den in Whitefriars, a disreputable area of London. There she meets Mother Red-Cap, the leader of the thieves, and Bess Columbine, who had been Black Jack's mistress before Amber came onto the scene.

Amber gives birth to a baby boy, whom she names Bruce, and Mother Red-Cap arranges for the child to be taken care of by Mrs. Chiverton, who lives in a village on the outskirts of London. Mother Red-Cap also employs a student, Michael Godfrey, to instruct Amber in the manners and speech of a London lady. The avaricious woman plans to use Amber as a decoy in her robbery schemes. Amber learns quickly and, masquerading as a lady of quality, lures unsuspecting men into the hands of Black Jack's gang. Tension between Amber and Bess becomes so great that Mother Red-Cap orders the latter to leave Whitefriars. Amber and Black Jack attempt to rob a wealthy gentleman whose coach has stopped off at a country inn but the vindictive Bess has informed the constables of the plan. Bess' plan backfires when Amber narrowly escapes and Black Jack is arrested and hanged.

Amber seeks refuge with Michael Godfrey and they briefly become lovers. Fearing that she will be arrested, Amber joins the company of His Majesty's Players, knowing that actors are under the protection of the King and exempt from the law. Once again Amber arouses the jealousy of another woman when she flirts with Capt. Rex Morgan, the admirer of actress Beck Marshall. Capt. Morgan quickly succumbs to Amber's charms and she becomes his mistress.

While watching King Charles' procession through London with his new Portuguese queen Catherine, Amber encounters Almsbury. Although he is now married with two children, he confesses that he loves her and they sleep together. One day, while Amber is riding in her coach to a rehearsal at the theatre, a young girl named Nan Britton approaches and asks for her protection. Nan has stolen a loaf of bread and the constables are after her. Remembering her days in Newgate Prison, Amber aids the girl and employs her as a maid. In no time at all they become fast friends.

King Charles takes notice of Amber at the theatre one evening and requests that she lay with him. She readily agrees and, for her favors, the King pays her fifty pounds. When Rex learns of her infidelity with Charles, he walks out on Amber, but he is so much in love with her that he returns and begs her to marry him. Bruce Carlton returns to London after two and a half years at sea and Amber is as smitten with him as ever. Amber takes Bruce to meet their son and then imprudently stays in the country with him. Upon her return she is confronted by a jealous Rex who challenges Bruce to a duel. The men meet at Marrowbone Fields for the confrontation. A heated sword fight ensues, ending when Bruce kills Rex as a horrified Amber looks on.

PART THREE

Following the death of Rex Morgan, Amber returns to the theatre where she is more popular and sought after by the fops than ever. She has a steady succession of lovers, including an unpleasant encounter with George Villiers, the rich and powerful Duke of Buckingham.

Unfortunately, she soon finds herself with child. She takes an abortive concoction and embarks on a journey to the spa at Tunbridge Wells. Amber hopes the medicine combined with the long, rough coach ride will rid her of the baby, which it does.

Along the way she encounters an older gentleman whose coach and horses have been stolen by highwaymen. His name is Samuel Dangerfield and Amber offers him a ride in her coach to Tunbridge. She learns that Mr. Dangerfield is a rich merchant and a widower so she sets her sights on marrying him. He easily falls prey to her allure. They marry and he brings her to the family mansion in London. Most of the family instantly hates her, especially the eldest daughter Lettice who considers Amber to be a hussy and a fortune hunter. Only the youngest daughter Jemima is willing to be congenial to Amber. Their friendship ends abruptly when Amber finds out that Jemima is in love with her father's business associate, the famous privateer Bruce Carlton.

When Bruce again returns to London, Amber and Jemima engage in a tug of war for his affections. Bruce and Amber begin a clandestine affair and once again she becomes pregnant. Amber is shocked to discover that Bruce has also been sleeping with Jemima and she too is carrying his child. Amber convinces Samuel to marry Jemima off to another man against her wishes. Samuel is overjoyed when he finds out that Amber is going to have a baby and she lets him believe that he is the father.

Samuel Dangerfield dies a few days before Amber's daughter Susanna is born, leaving his widow and the child a considerable fortune. To the great relief of the family, Amber moves out of Dangerfield House and takes fashionable lodgings at the Plume of Feathers in St. Martin's Lane. When the Great Plague of 1665 begins to sweep through London, the populace starts to flee the city in droves. Amber is told that Bruce has just put into port again. After sending Nan, Susanna, and the servants out of London to escape the pestilence, she goes to the docks in search of him.

PART FOUR

Amber finds a weary Bruce supervising the unloading of his ships. She takes him back to her lodgings for supper but, as the evening progresses, he begins to exhibit unmistakable symptoms of plague. Bruce's health rapidly deteriorates and he develops the dread plague boil. Although he implores Amber to leave, she refuses to abandon him. Amber enlists the aid of a doctor who offers her little hope regarding Bruce's condition. He sends along a parish nurse, Mrs. Spong, to assist Amber and the old woman proves to be a drunkard who is more trouble than help. Bruce's boil finally breaks but, just as he is beginning to regain his health, Mrs. Spong falls sick and dies.

As Bruce is recovering Amber realizes that she too has contracted the Plague. Soon she is gravely ill and Mrs. Sykes, another parish nurse, arrives to help the convalescing Bruce take care of her. Amber also develops a plague boil but it refuses to break. Bruce and Mrs. Sykes lance the boil and Amber's condition seems to improve slightly. Mrs. Sykes comes down with the Plague and, in her agony, jumps from a window to her death. Yet another parish nurse arrives to help Bruce care for Amber. This is the aptly named Mrs. Maggot, whose only concern is to rob her helpless patients even if she has to murder them to do it. While Amber lies in a near coma, Mrs. Maggot attempts to strangle Bruce with a noose, but he manages to get it around her neck and kills her instead.

When Amber has sufficiently recovered to travel, Bruce takes the yacht from the dock at Almsbury House and they sail up the Thames to Barberry Hill, the Almsbury country estate. There they are reunited with little Bruce who now lives with Almsbury and his wife Emily. Almsbury sends out some men to locate Nan and Susanna and bring them back to Barberry Hill. The idyllic days she has spent with Bruce sailing on the Thames have convinced Amber that he truly loves her and will marry her at last. She broaches the subject but he tells her that he will shortly be returning to London and intends to go alone. The next day he takes his leave without even saying goodbye to her. She attempts to follow him on horseback but Almsbury prevents her from doing so.

A new houseguest arrives at Barberry Hill. It is Edmund Mortimer, Earl of Radclyffe. Although outwardly he shows little interest in her, Almsbury assures Amber that Radclyffe is quite taken with her as she reminds him of a woman from his past. Having lost his family fortune in the Wars, Radclyffe is also interested in the sixty-six-thousand pounds Amber has accumulated. Despite finding him old and unappealing, the prospect of becoming a countess intrigues Amber. Reckoning that it is worth sharing her wealth to acquire a title, Amber marries Radclyffe and they move into his dilapidated house just outside the City Gates of London. Amber goes to her goldsmith Shadrac Newbold to check on her finances and he tells her that two weeks prior Bruce set sail for America.

Amber soon realizes what a hard bargain she has made to gain a title. Radclyffe is impotent and a profligate spender of her money. Her dream of being presented at Court is realized when she and Radclyffe are invited to a royal ball at Whitehall. Her presence causes a sensation and even

King Charles flaunts protocol by asking her to dance. Her triumph is short lived when a jealous Radclyffe forces her to join him in an early departure.

Although Radclyffe attempts to keep Amber a virtual prisoner in their home, another invitation arrives from Whitehall and the Earl cannot ignore the King's request. At Court, Amber is more popular than ever and Charles makes it plain that he eventually intends to bed her. To thwart this, Radclyffe drugs and binds Amber and takes her to his country estate, Lime Park, where his son Philip lives with his wife Jenny. To amuse herself and to get revenge on Radclyffe, Amber seduces Philip and they begin an affair. A few weeks later, the Earl goes off to London on business and will not allow Amber to accompany him. She is so furious at being left behind that she shuts herself up in her rooms, refusing to eat. That night Philip is suddenly taken ill and, before dying, tells Amber that he believes his food had been poisoned. Amber realizes that Radclyffe attempted to kill them both and only her refusal of food has saved her.

Determined to be rid of Radclyffe once and for all, Amber dresses as a man and sets off on horseback to London accompanied by her faithful servant Big John Waterman and four other men. Along the way they hear of a tremendous fire which is burning out of control in London. Amber and the men arrive to find themselves in the midst of a chaotic exodus from the burning city. At Radclyffe House Amber surprises the Earl, who is supervising the packing of his belongings. She confronts him with the murder of his son and he attempts to strike her with a candlestick. Big John intervenes, knocking the Earl unconscious. At this moment the house catches fire and Amber flees, leaving the unconscious Radclyffe to perish in the conflagration.

PART FIVE

Three and a half months after the death of Radclyffe, Amber returns to London, which is still recovering from the Great Fire. Although her late husband's spending has reduced her fortune to twenty-eight-thousand pounds, she is still one of the richest women in England. When Amber returns to Whitehall, her appearance is greeted with great enthusiasm by the gentlemen of the Court and especially by King Charles, who quickly makes her his mistress. Not so enthusiastic is Barbara Palmer, Countess of Castlemaine, whose position as Charles' favorite has slipped considerably. Soon Amber finds herself pregnant with Charles' baby. The King insists she marry Gerald Stanhope, one of the more innocuous courtiers, to give

the child the benefit of a surname. To make the union more acceptable
to both parties, he makes Gerald the Earl of Danforth. Although now
married, Amber is living at Almsbury House and Gerald has taken lodgings in Covent Garden. When his mother, Lady Lucilla Stanhope, hears
of this outrage she comes immediately to London to try and remedy the
situation. Not long after her arrival, Bruce returns to England.

   Bruce and Amber take up where they had left off and their passion for
each other is stronger than ever. But Bruce confesses to Amber that he is
married and has a child. Although she is heartbroken, Amber realizes that,
wife or not, he is as infatuated with her as ever. Lady Stanhope continues
to be a thorn in Amber's side; spending Amber's money and forcing her
son's unwanted attentions on his recalcitrant wife. One night Gerald
unexpectedly comes into Amber's bedroom and catches her with Bruce.

   When the Dutch invade England, Bruce and Almsbury ride off to
help defend their country. Although the rest of the household flees to
the country, Amber decides to stay in London and wait for Bruce to
return. A peace treaty is signed and Bruce becomes impatient to return
to America. He asks Amber if he can take their son with him. At first
she refuses but later relents when she realizes how much the boy loves
his father. As Bruce and their son set sail, Amber watches from the pier
with an aching heart.

   About a month after Bruce's departure, Amber is appointed a Lady
of the Bedchamber and moves into Whitehall. Soon after, she is delivered of a male child whom she names Charles, after his father. Lady
Stanhope continues to plague her for money and Amber finally marries
her off to a young fop with a bribe of five thousand pounds. She makes
a similar arrangement with Gerald, offering him four hundred pounds
a year if he will trouble her no more. In addition to her great wealth
Amber now has position at Court as well, but she still doesn't have the
one thing she really desires: Bruce Carlton. She confesses her longings
to Almsbury who tells her that, were it not for Bruce, he would have
asked her to marry him.

   Charles finally ends his relationship with Castlemaine once and for all.
Castlemaine's cousin, the Duke of Buckingham, wastes no time in seeking
out Amber. He hopes to ally himself with the woman most likely to have
the greatest influence at Whitehall. Amber is suspicious of his motives but
pretends to go along with his offer of friendship. Buckingham hatches
a scheme to get rid of Queen Catherine but Amber, who is fond of the
lady, exposes the plot thereby incurring the Duke's enmity. Immediately
Charles' Secretary of State, Baron Arlington, seeks to ingratiate himself

with Amber. Arlington is a bitter enemy of Buckingham and believes that Amber can be of use in obtaining incriminating evidence to bring about the Duke's downfall.

As a proof of his goodwill, Arlington convinces Charles to confer on Amber the title of Duchess of Ravenspur.

PART SIX

Over two years have passed since Amber first came back to the Court and, befitting her title of Duchess, she decides to build the grandest and most gaudy house in London. One day, while she is overseeing the construction of Ravenspur House, Almsbury comes to tell her that Bruce, his wife Corinna, their young daughter, and little Bruce arrived in London the night before. They will be attending a ball at the home of Baron Arlington in a few days. Amber realizes that she must do something to outshine Bruce's wife so she sets her dressmaker to creating a gown the likes of which no one has dared wear before.

Amber arrives at the ball wearing her new gown, which is cut so that her breasts are completely exposed. The courtiers, including King Charles, are scandalized and Amber realizes that she has made a terrible mistake. When Lady Carlton arrives with her husband, everyone is impressed by her serene beauty, modesty, and unaffected charm. Her presence far eclipses that of Amber.

Several days later, Almsbury brings Bruce to Amber's rooms so he can see his daughter Susanna. At first, Bruce remains aloof but, when Almsbury takes his leave, Bruce stays and makes love to Amber. The next afternoon Bruce brings little Bruce to see his mother. After that he visits Amber often, with or without their son. News of the affair becomes the gossip of the Court but Lady Carlton appears to be unaware of the situation. One day Amber pays a courtesy call on Corinna, who reveals that she and Bruce are going to have another child, their infant son having died the year before of smallpox. Although she is jealous, Amber is secure in her love for Bruce.

As time passes Corinna begins to have her suspicions about Bruce and his relationship with the Duchess of Ravenspur. These suspicions are confirmed when the Countess of Castlemaine visits her, armed with the latest gossip about her husband and Amber. That night Corinna confronts Bruce and he confesses that he has known Amber for ten years and that little Bruce is their son. He also tells her that he never thought of Amber as a wife, only a mistress. He promises Corinna that the affair is over.

Bruce abruptly stops seeing Amber, with no explanation to her what-soever. With the help of Almsbury, Amber manages to meet Bruce in private and, once again, he succumbs to his desire for her. He rents apart-ments in a lodging house and they meet there often, with Amber taking great care to go in disguise so no one will know of their romance. Ravens-pur House is finally completed and Amber gives a lavish party which is a great success.

For five months Amber and Bruce continue to meet in secret. But as the time for his departure to America draws closer, Amber grows increas-ingly discontent with their arrangement. When she finally confronts him with her unhappiness about the situation, he says goodbye and walks out on her for good. A week after their quarrel, Amber attends an auction where Corinna bids on length of rare Indian Calico. Out of spite, Amber attempts to outbid her but at the last moment Bruce intervenes and wins the Calico for his wife. Amber is publicly humiliated, to the joy of her envious peers. Amber manages to arrange one last meeting alone with Bruce and his cold rejection makes her realize he is finally done with her. In a fury of desperation and rage, Amber goes to see Corinna and taunts her with Bruce's infidelity, but Corinna refuses to be baited and calmly dismisses her. Bruce walks in during the confrontation and his anger is so great that he nearly strangles Amber to death. The excitement causes Corinna to go into labor and Bruce tells Amber to leave.

Amber goes into seclusion until one day she is visited by the Duke of Buckingham. He gives her twenty-five-thousand pounds to assist him in a plot to poison Baron Arlington and promises to pay her a like amount if the plan succeeds. Amber agrees and then goes to Arlington demanding five thousand pounds for information she has regarding an attempt on his life. When Buckingham discovers what has happened and confronts her, Amber tells him that unless he leaves her alone she will inform King Charles of his nefarious intrigues.

Amber learns that Corinna delivered a son the day of their last encoun-ter and that she and Bruce will soon be sailing for France, then on to their home in Virginia. Amber sees Almsbury at Court and he refuses to discuss Bruce with her. She realizes that what she did has turned Alms-bury against her. The day of Bruce's departure, Amber goes to Almsbury House to waylay him but when he sees her he will say no more than a cool farewell. Determined to get even with Amber for betraying him, Buckingham joins forces with Arlington in a cabal to get rid of her once and for all. The day after Bruce and Corinna set sail, a note is delivered to Amber saying that Lady Carlton took sick on the channel crossing and died. Amber wastes no time in booking passage for herself and her retinue on a ship bound for America. As Buckingham and Arlington are congratulating themselves on the success of their scheme, Amber boards a coach bound for the docks and leaves Whitehall forever.

CHAPTER THREE

From Novel to Film

THE ADAPTATION OF ANY NOVEL TO FILM IS PROBLEMATIC
in the best of circumstances. Taking one form of artistic expression and
making it conform to the dictates of another is a singular challenge if the
integrity of both is to be retained. Turning a novel as popular as *Forever
Amber* into a movie came with its own special set of problems. There was
tremendous audience expectation and trepidation. How could they possibly include all of the important aspects of the plot, characters, and sexual
situations? In regard to the latter, any filmmaker who undertook this project knew the censor would be looking over his shoulder throughout. The
length and scope of the story was also daunting. But the potential money
to be made from such an endeavor often makes motion picture studios
throw all caution to the winds. The writing of a script is seldom done
without considerable effort but few have had the lengthy and troubled
gestation period of *Forever Amber*, with eight different versions of the
screenplay being written by a trio of writers.

Five weeks before the publication of *Forever Amber*, an undisclosed
movie studio had already shown interest in acquiring the film rights based
only on a synopsis of the story. The Hays Office, who saw to it that the
studios adhered to the Production Code they had established, was already
sniffing out this potentially offensive material. While the novel was still
in galleys, the Hays Office discouraged any bidding by producers for the
motion picture rights to *Forever Amber*. In the meantime, Macmillan
Company had engaged literary agent Annie Laurie Williams to represent
Kathleen Winsor. Ms. Williams had become famous as "the agent who
sold *Gone with the Wind* to the movies." She was well known with the
studios for her abilities to pick out properties that had motion picture
potential. Both MGM and 20th Century-Fox approached Joseph Breen
at the Production Code Administration with the idea of a film adaptation.
Breen informed them that the PCA had "officially banned the novel from
motion picture consideration" based on the controversial nature of the
subject matter. Fox persisted and on October 3, 1944, their Public Relations Director, Col. Jason Joy, sent Breen a synopsis of the novel. Breen
respond the following day saying: "We have read with great care the 48
page synopsis…and I am hastening to advise you that it is our considered
unanimous judgment that this story is utterly and completely unacceptable under any one of a dozen provisions of the Production Code. As we
read it, this story, is hardly more than a saga of illicit sex and adultery into
which enters the elements of bastardy, perversion, impotency, pregnancy,
abortion, murder and marriage without even the slightest suggestion of
compensating moral values."

On October 11, only a few days prior to the novel's official release, the *New York Herald* ran an article entitled "Charles II Annal Too Hot for Films." The article states that the Hays Office "has intimated to Hollywood that it does not think the love life of Charles II and the fecundity of the Restoration period is proper fare for movie goers." The article concludes with a comment by Kathleen Winsor: "The whole thing, this attitude of the Hays Office, is absurd. Can it be that they want history rewritten for popular tastes?"

But Darryl F. Zanuck, Head of Production at Fox, was not one to be easily dissuaded once he had set his mind on something. On November 2, Fox paid $10 for an exclusive option (to expire on January 15, 1945) to acquire the motion picture rights to *Forever Amber*. The asking price was $125,000. If an excess of 400,000 copies of the book were sold, the price would then increase to not more than $200,000. On December 27, Zanuck advised the Fox legal department that he wanted to take up the option on *Forever Amber*. This was a tremendous amount of money to be paid for the screen rights to a novel. Zanuck had only offered $35,000 for *Gone with the Wind* and it had eventually been sold to David O. Selznick for $50,000.

On January 4, 1945, Fox sent a letter to Kathleen Winsor accepting her offer to sell the rights to them for $125,000 and four days later the contract was signed. On February 21, an Inter-office Correspondence was issued by the Fox legal department stating: "Please be advised that we have exercised our option and have purchased the worldwide silent, sound, dialogue and talking motion picture rights in and to *Forever Amber*, an original novel, by Kathleen Winsor."

Fox issued statements claiming that the contract for the screen rights contained a clause which stated that payment to Ms. Winsor was to be withheld until the production began filming. Therefore, if the studio was unable to prepare an acceptable screen treatment, the rights would revert back to the author. The studio also said the contract stipulated that she would serve as a consultant on the production. In a 1988 correspondence with Ms. Winsor she discredited these statements as publicity generated by the studio. Examination of the original contract confirmed that she was correct. She also maintained that she was never consulted on any aspects of the actual production or casting. However, her opinion was briefly sought on the first version of the screenplay.

In early 1945, Zanuck assigned Jerome Cady to adapt the novel's 972 pages into a workable screenplay. He had previously written some of the Lupe Velez Mexican Spitfire films for RKO and Mr. Moto and Charlie Chan scripts at Fox. Cady had recently been nominated for the Academy

Award for Best Original Screenplay for Fox's *A Wing and a Prayer* (1944). He had also made some uncredited contributions to the script of *Laura* (1944). Otherwise, he would probably have not been seriously considered as screenwriter for such a high-profile production as *Forever Amber*.

Although he would continue to closely supervise all aspects of this important production, Darryl Zanuck named William Perlberg as producer. Perlberg had previously produced, among other films, *The Song of Bernadette* (1943) for Fox. This was another movie which had been adapted from a popular and lengthy novel. It had turned out to be a tremendous success for the studio so Zanuck felt that the production was in capable hands. Nevertheless, the final word on *Forever Amber* was always Darryl Zanuck's. As a former screenwriter, Zanuck, more than any other studio head of his time, understood the importance of a good script. In his biography of Zanuck, *Don't Say Yes Until I Finish Talking*, Mel Gussow says of the mogul: "He himself began as a writer but his contribution to the movies has not been as a writer but as an editor, as a recognizer of writing that works, as a catalyst for rewriting that works better." Anticipating problems with the censors, but not wanting to disappoint fans of the novel, Zanuck sent a memo to Jerome Cady which said in part: "I believe we will be severely criticized if we definitely prove that Amber does not sleep with every man she is supposed to sleep with. It would be a crime to whitewash Amber and mathematically and statistically prove that she is a perpetual virgin. There should be nothing in our script which can be used as concrete evidence one way or the other."

The task of turning such a massive novel into an acceptable screenplay would be not an easy one. The wealth of historical details and events present in the book was nearly overwhelming, as were the multitude of characters weaving in and out of the plot. In the book, Amber has four husbands, three children, and no less than fourteen lovers who are mentioned by name. In accordance with Zanuck's directives, Jerome Cady was to select only those persons and events which were crucial to the main plot line, but also be careful not to palliate the character of Amber.

Jerome Cady's first step was to write a 189-page "Treatment" of the novel, which is dated March 19, 1945. In it he includes, verbatim, a great deal of Kathleen Winsor's descriptions and dialogue. Almost all of the characters, both major and minor, are present as well as the inclusion of some unneeded situations and details. There are also major alterations to the story; some are well done (the prologue) and others are downright awful (the ending). It should be noted that John Randolph, Earl of Almsbury would become "Lord Harry Almsbury" in all of versions of the script. The following are changes to the original story that Cady made in his adaptation.

The Treatment opens with a Prologue set in 1644. A coach bares the crest of the Earl of Rosswood. Inside it are John Mainwaring, his baby daughter, and a nurse. The coach halts at the village of Marygreen where Mainwaring leaves the infant with Matthew and Sarah Goodegroome. Shortly after Mainwaring departs, Edmund Mortimer, the Earl of Radclyffe, arrives. Radclyffe vindictively removes the lavaliere with a portrait of her mother from around the baby's neck so that she will never know the truth of her noble parentage. He takes his leave, vowing that John Mainwaring will never live to return and reclaim his daughter. Sarah Goodegroome names the baby Amber, after her amber-colored eyes.

The story resumes sixteen years later at a May Fair in Marygreen. The descriptions, dialogue, and events are all taken directly from the book until Bruce takes Amber to London. In this version they arrive on the day of Charles Stuart's Restoration Coronation Procession. After Bruce departs London, a pregnant Amber goes to an astrologer, who quickly informs Sally Goodman and Luke Channel about the money Bruce has given Amber. Sally and Luke arrange for two ruffians to accost Amber and Luke intervenes to save her. Out of gratitude, Amber invites Sally and Luke to supper at her lodgings. They drug Amber's wine and rob her of everything.

The section in Newgate Prison is per the novel with the exception of an elaborate escape plan concocted between Black Jack and Mrs. Cleggat. The Whitefriars and Michael Godfrey segments of the story are without change other than Nan Britton being introduced as a ladies maid backstage at the theatre where Amber gains employment. After the death of Rex Morgan, Amber takes her son to Tunbridge Wells where she meets Samuel Dangerfield. There is a cut from a "Record of Marriage" for Amber and Samuel to Amber dressed as a widow conferring with her goldsmith Shadrac Newbold. She is converting the financial holdings that Samuel left her into gold. The Plague scenes are as in the book except that the three parish nurses are condensed into "Mrs. Spong." Most of the Radclyffe scenes are close to the source but herein Radclyffe dies with the lavaliere of Amber's mother clutched in his hand.

Amber returns to Whitehall and becomes the mistress of King Charles. Charles makes her the "Dutchess of Ravenspur" (Amber's last husband,

Gerald Stanhope, is not included in the treatment). The remainder of the adaptation includes elements from the book but with different emphasis. Amber goes to an astrologer and overhears a plan by the Duke of Buckingham and the Countess of Castlemaine to get rid of the Queen and have Castlemaine take her place. Amber manages to get proof of the plot in writing.

Bruce returns to London accompanied by a young woman named Corinna. He comes to Amber and asks her to let him take their son back to America but she refuses. At an auction, Amber vindictively bids against Corinna for some expensive cloth. Bruce intervenes and buys it for Corinna. Determined to overshadow the pretty newcomer, Amber attends a palace ball wearing a scandalously revealing gown (bare midriff, rather than bare-breasted as in the novel). Charles is shocked at her behavior and orders her to leave Whitehall permanently. She attempts to win back his favor by presenting the evidence of the plot against his Queen. Charles refuses to forgive her but offers to grant her one last boon. Amber tells him that she wants to marry Bruce. Charles sends for Bruce who informs them that he cannot comply to the request, revealing that he is already wed to Corinna. Amber has now lost all hope of ever marrying the man she loves and has lost the favor of the King as well. She agrees to let Bruce take their son to America.

In the final scene, Amber goes alone to the docks to watch the ship carrying Bruce, Corinna, and Little Bruce sail away. The last shot is a close up of Amber's plumed hat floating on the water (presumably she has drowned herself). FADE OUT

From this lengthy treatment, Jerome Cady wrote a 1st Draft Continuity Script (May 1, 1945). After reading the script, Darryl Zanuck sent a memo dated May 18 to Cady and William Perlberg. He said, "Script is way over length. At least thirty to forty pages have got to come out." He also adds that at its present length the film would run about 30 reels. Zanuck goes on to say: "My first major criticism has to do with the character of Amber. She never got under my skin for one minute. I never believed her nor did I believe anything about her, nor did I understand her. I honestly believe that the whole key to the success of this film largely depends on whether or not we are able to convincingly sell Amber to an audience. This script does not sell her to me. Once we have solidly set the foundation and groundwork of Amber's character I know that despite the fact she is at times a bitch, and despite the fact that at times she is ruthless, viciously ambitious, and even promiscuous if being promiscuous will bring her fame and riches, nevertheless in spite of all this we will root for her and be in sympathy with what she is doing."

His second criticism is that there is too much narrative and not enough dramatization. Zanuck breaks the script into a prologue and seven acts, one act for each of the men in Amber's life. He also lists what it is she hopes to gain by her relationship with each of them:

1. *Bruce Carlton — Love*
2. *Black Jack — Freedom*
3. *Michael Godfrey — Safety*
4. *Rex Morgan — Money*
5. *Sam Dangerfield — Riches*
6. *Earl of Radclyffe — Title*
7. *King Charles — Position and Fame*

Cady's attempts to remain faithful to the structure of the original book did not please Zanuck. The memo goes on to say: "If you are true to the spirit of a book and reasonably accurate with the characters, it does not matter a tinker's damn whether or not you faithfully follow the continuity or structure of the book, providing, of course, you do not leave out any of the outstanding moments of the book. If we are to succeed, we must adroitly select what we are going to tell. By concentrating on these selected elements…we will come out with a powerfully dramatic story." Zanuck stressed this policy whenever Fox writers adapted long novels into screenplays. Other Fox films such as *How Green Was My Valley* (1941), *Captain from Castile* (1947) and *The Egyptian* (1954) are all true to the spirit of the original book, without slavishly including every character and plot device in the story.

A Story Conference between Zanuck, Cady, and Perlberg was held on June 13 to discuss the 1st Draft Continuity Script. Zanuck brought up three major points:

1. *Amber's character*
2. *Amber's motives*
3. *"Forget narrative and concentrate on a compact dramatization"*

He also "suggested" the elimination of three scenes: the May Fair at Marygreen, the Restoration Procession, and a scene where Charles gives Amber gold after she spends the night with him. The first two were obviously budgetary considerations as both scenes would require crowds of extras. The last was made with the comment, "Messrs. Perlberg and Cady: You don't <u>really</u> think the Hays Office will let you get away with this do you?"

William Perlberg sent a copy of Cady's 1st Draft script to Kathleen Winsor, asking for her comments. According to Perlberg, "She didn't seem to understand our problems. She objected to the fact that we referred to 'Lady Castlemaine' at a point in the script where, she said, Castlemaine hadn't received her title yet and was still Barbara Palmer. We were just a year out, but that seemed to bother her a lot." Her advice was never asked again throughout the production. Kathleen Winsor later confessed that her greatest complaint about the script was that it had eliminated most of the section of the book where Amber is married to her second husband, Samuel Dangerfield. She said, "No story of the Restoration period can be complete without showing the power and respectability of the merchant princes. I don't see how they can fail to see the importance of the Dangerfield sequence."

Jerome Cady submitted a Revised Temporary Draft (July 13, 1945), but after reading it Zanuck apparently lost all faith in Cady's abilities to provide him with a suitable script. In August 1945 he removed Cady from the project and assigned the rewrite to Philip Dunne. Dunne, one of Fox's best writers, had recently returned to the studio after four years of producing overseas propaganda films for the Office of War Information. Dunne was reluctant to accept the assignment of working on *Forever Amber* as he wanted to write "significant pictures, high-minded films," but Zanuck insisted. In his autobiography, *Take Two*, Dunne said, "The script Zanuck handed me to rewrite was perfectly terrible, but at that it was an improvement on the book, so I can't blame my predecessor." Dunne thought the whole project was so hopeless that he proposed to Zanuck that he rewrite it as a "satirical comedy." Since nothing could have been further from Zanuck's intention to remain faithful to the spirit of the book, the suggestion was immediately dismissed.

Philip Dunne submitted a 2nd Draft Continuity Script (August 30, 1945), which includes a number of significant changes from the Cady script. Both the Prologue and the scenes with Sally Goodman and Luke Channel were eliminated entirely. Amber now meets Nan Britton in Newgate Prison. All of Moll Turner's dialogue has been cut, but the characters of Mrs. Cleggat and Bess Columbine are retained. After the failed coach robbery and the death of Black Jack, Amber goes through the open door of a building as she attempts to hide from the law. She collapses in a faint and the next morning is found by Edward Kynaston, Beck Marshall, and Thomas Killigrew. She has stumbled into the Theatre Royal and Almsbury, who is a friend of Killigrew, convinces him to hire her as an actress. The script retains the Tunbridge Wells sequence and expands the Samuel Dangerfield episode to include Lettice and the family, but not his daughter Jemima. The character of Big John has also been retained. The death of Radclyffe is much closer to that in the final film version as is Amber's scheming which alienates Charles' affections. Corinna comes to Amber and asks her to give up Bruce and allow Little Bruce to come with them to America. Impressed by her obvious sincerity, Amber agrees and later expresses her regrets to Nan:

> *Amber:* "Nan, I suppose I've been very wicked…and I suppose I should have expected punishment."

This script ends with Bruce and Little Bruce driving away in a carriage, very much the same as in what would become the final censored version of the film.

On September 4, Zanuck called in Dunne and Perlberg for a Story Conference on the 2nd Draft Continuity. Zanuck suggested that the Samuel Dangerfield character be eliminated and that Amber should marry Rex Morgan instead. After he dies in the duel, she will then inherit his money. He also made the following comment regarding the ending: "We should finish the picture along these lines: Amber stares after the departing figures of Bruce and her son, then goes to her dressing-table, sits down and stares at herself in the mirror. CAMERA COMES IN to a Close Shot which fills the entire screen, of Amber's reflection in the mirror, with tears running down her cheeks. Finis."

Dunne next submitted a Temporary Draft Script (September 26, 1945). The major change in this version is that it opens with Amber in a bathtub looking at her reflection in a small, cracked mirror. Zanuck responded to this with a memo saying: "I do not like opening with Amber in bathtub. This is just the kind of thing the critics would love to hurl at us or kid us about because of DeMille, etc." Oddly, the Samuel Dangerfield scenes are still included despite Zanuck's previous suggestion to remove them. At the end, Corinna comes to Amber to ask for Little Bruce. Corinna agrees that he shall have his father's title of "Lord" even if they have another son. Per Zanuck's suggestion, the last shot is of Amber looking at herself in a mirror, crying. This Temporary Draft Script was submitted to the Production Code Administration on October 9, 1945, with a message from Zanuck saying that he believes that the script "has preserved a great deal of the spirit of the original material and yet has managed to avoid distasteful or censorable elements." Joseph Breen disagreed, saying that although Zanuck "has done a tremendous job in an endeavor to establish a screenplay from this material, we felt that he has not done enough and that the material, in its present form, was not acceptable from the standpoint of the Code."

On October 16, Zanuck sent a memo to Philip Dunne and William Perlberg regarding a conference he had with Joseph Breen of the PCA: "Breen is very pleased by the general handling of the story. He will accept the fact of the illegitimate child providing...

1. Almsbury becomes the "Voice of Morality throughout the balance of the picture."

2. "Work into the dialogue a note of self-condemnation from Bruce."

3. It must be made clear at the finish "that Amber does not triumph by having her child get Bruce's title."

The changes in the Final Draft Script (October 27, 1945) consist mainly of a new opening with Amber looking at herself in a small mirror which she then buys from a Gypsy peddler, and dialogue revisions which eliminate all references to "Bruce's title" in the final scene. Almsbury is also provided with a brief "Voice of Morality" speech:

Almsbury: "We live in an evil age. Perhaps none in all past history has been so evil, no city reached the depths that London has reached today."

Although the film version of *Forever Amber* was on its second writer, a director had not yet been named. Zanuck had narrowed the choices down to Edmund Goulding and John M. Stahl. Gene Tierney, who worked with both, discusses their very different approaches to filmmaking in her autobiography, *Self-Portrait*. She says that Goulding was easygoing and worked closely with his performers in a non-threatening way, creating a cheerful atmosphere on the set. Stahl, on the other hand, could be a "taskmaster" although he "had a reputation for bringing out the best in an actress."

In October 1945, while the PCA was busy scrutinizing Philip Dunne's latest screenplay, *The Hollywood Reporter* announced that John M. Stahl had been selected as director. Stahl had recently completed Leave *Her to Heaven*, based on a very successful novel which revolved around an extremely unsympathetic female character. This announcement may have been premature because as late as February 1, 1946, the *Los Angeles Examiner* listed Edmund Goulding as the director of *Forever Amber*. If Goulding really was still in the running, the January 1946 release of *Leave Her to Heaven* soon changed Zanuck's mind. To quote film historian Rudy Behlmer, "*Leave Her to Heaven* made more money than any Fox picture up to that time by a wide margin." Stahl was also able to coax an Oscar-worthy performance from star Gene Tierney. These two factors would obviously have influenced Zanuck greatly in his final choice of John Stahl for director. Previously, Stahl and producer William Perlberg had worked well together on Fox's *The Eve of St. Mark* (1944), which was another plus factor to be considered.

On November 23, Fox's legal department received a letter from The Macmillan Company informing them that the novel had sold 897,366 copies to date. Kathleen Winsor was now to be paid an additional $75,000 per the clause in the original contract.

A Revised Final Script (December 18, 1945) was submitted to the PCA. Philip Dunne said, "After several weeks of uninspired work, I turned in a dreary, dutifully sanitized script," which was fully approved by the PCA in December 1945. Notes from Zanuck propose that the "Mistress Spong incident" be removed along with the entire Dangerfield episode. He also suggests that Big John replace Radclyffe's manservant "Guido." Three other changes distinguish this from previous scripts:

1. Amber goes to Almsbury at the Saracen's Head Inn after she escapes from the constables following the attempted coach robbery. Almsbury uses his influence to find her employment in the theatre.

2. Amber walks in on Nan and Big John at her Plume of Feathers apartment. They are fearful of the plague and beg Amber to leave London.

3. Amber pays Wilmot, a notorious pamphleteer, to write a doggerel about herself and Bruce Carlton. It makes Charles look a fool so he banishes her from Whitehall.

As the New Year began and the reality of a film version of *Forever Amber* was looming in the not-too-distant future, the "Voices of Morality" throughout the nation began to rally against this terrible inequity.

Hollywood gossip reporter Jimmie Fidler was one of the earliest to vent his spleen in his syndicated column of January 16,1946: "No matter how thoroughly 20th Century-Fox succeeds in 'cleaning up' Kathleen Winsor's sexsational novel, its production, in my opinion, will still be a black eye to the motion picture industry. A studio which is capable of producing a 'Song of Bernadette' has no need to make a 'Forever Amber.'" Letters and petitions of protest began to flood the PCA and Fox from such organizations as the San Francisco Motion Picture Council, the Los Angeles Tenth District California Congress of Parents and Teachers, and from nearly every branch of the National Council of Catholic Women in the country. The Huntington, Indiana Legion of Decency sent 125 postcards to Col. Jason Joy at Fox protesting the "producing and showing of the film *Forever Amber*." In addition to letters from organizations, hundreds of pieces of correspondence from distressed individuals were sent as well. A typical example of these came from Bernard J. Mann an "American Citizen!" in Bangor, Maine: "Why should we allow filthy motion pictures to appear to befoul and tarnish the minds of our darling youngsters any more than we should allow them to eat hot dogs which are rotten or spoiled. Down with such stinking pictures as *Forever Amber!*"

A curious article in the February 9, 1946, edition of *Motion Picture Herald* reported that "a script which had some loose relation to the novel" had been approved by the Motion Picture Association but the forthcoming film would not present the story written by Kathleen Winsor. The title would be used solely for "merchandising reasons." Later, when William Perlberg was asked about whether any of the book remained in the screenplay he replied, "It's all there. The production code does not object to promiscuity, as long as it is punished." Pointing out the similarities between his heroine and Scarlett O'Hara, Perlberg went on to say, "*Forever Amber* will be an even greater preachment against selfishness than *Gone with the Wind*. The theme is that crime doesn't pay." Director John M. Stahl affirmed that Philip Dunne's screenplay was an extremely faithful adaptation of the novel and added, "You can do anything on the screen if you do it in good taste." Dunne added, "I don't see how any script could be that censorable. We had a scene when Bruce and the cavaliers were drinking wine. Mr. Breen's comment was, 'Watch that belch!' You see, a belch can be shown in pictures, but you aren't supposed to hear it. That makes it offensive."

Despite the approval of the PCA, the screenplay continued to be altered. Zanuck approved further changes on February 14. The Dangerfield sequence was shortened drastically. Also, during the Great Fire scene, Amber hits Radclyffe with a bag of jewels which spill out on the floor. Big John strikes Radclyffe down and then carries Amber from the burning building.

Philip Dunne next completed a Shooting Final Script (February 22, 1946). It does not include the 1644 prologue and the Dangerfield sequence has now been completely eliminated. Instead, after the death of Rex Morgan, the lawyer Newbold informs Amber that she has inherited his fortune. Big John is now shown as Amber's manservant but he has no dialogue in this version of the script. A revision dated March 12 provides a new opening for the film: A 17th-century-styled miniature portrait of the actress who will play Amber is surrounded by miniatures of the actors who will portray the men in her life. The first scene is now of Amber watching Bruce and his Cavaliers ride into Marygreen.

On April 2, 1946, Zanuck held a Story Conference with John M. Stahl, Philip Dunne, and William Perlberg. He suggested that the film open with a Gypsy telling Amber's fortune ("Men will fall in love with you — many men"). This new scene ends as the Cavaliers arrive in Marygreen. Later, Bruce is undecided about taking Amber to London:

> *Almsbury:* "Take her Bruce. She's good company. And she'll be no trouble."
> *Bruce:* "<u>Be</u> no trouble!? She <u>is</u> trouble!"

Unfortunately, this would prove to be an all-too-prophetic bit of dialogue.

CHAPTER FOUR

Almost Amber

from Fox and became a Colonel on active duty in the Army overseas for nine months. The European war ended in May 1945 and a few weeks later General Dwight D. Eisenhower invited Zanuck and eleven other Hollywood moguls to visit Europe. For two weeks they viewed the devastation that had been wrought, including the concentration camp at Dachau. Afterwards, Zanuck decided to go on to England, a country just beginning to recover from the effects of the War.

In London he attended the West End production of *Junior Miss*. The play had been very popular during the War and continued to be performed though out the blitz. Making her West End debut in the role of "Fuffy" was a nineteen-year-old Welsh-born and Dublin-raised actress named Peggy Cummins. Zanuck was very impressed by Miss Cummins and thought she would be perfect for the role of spoiled society girl "Betty Cream" in the forthcoming Fox production of *Cluny Brown*. Cummins had appeared in several movies in England, so she was no stranger to film acting when Zanuck signed her to a Fox contract and arranged for her to come to Hollywood. During his London sojourn Zanuck also signed on Rex Harrison, stipulating that his first film would be *Anna and the King of Siam*.

Darryl F. Zanuck with Peggy Cummins and Rex Harrison.

Meanwhile back at the studio, the big question was "Who will be Amber?" It was going to be difficult finding a counterpart for Kathleen Winsor's description: "Her honey-coloured hair fell in heavy waves below her shoulders and as she stared up at him her eyes, clear, speckled amber, seemed to tilt at the corners; her brows were black and swept up in arcs, and she had thick black lashes. There was about her a kind of warm

Michael Rennie, Margaret Lockwood, and Patricia Roc in The Wicked Lady.

luxuriance, something immediately suggestive to the men of pleasurable fulfillment — something for which she was not responsible but of which she was acutely conscious."

Both Vivien Leigh and Margaret Lockwood were approached to play Amber and both turned it down. Ms. Lockwood instead chose to play another Restoration lady of questionable morals in the British Gainsborough production of Madalen King-Hall's 1944 novel *The Life and Death of the Wicked Lady Skelton.* Inexpensively made and shot in only twelve days, *The Wicked Lady* (1945) was a big box-office success in England. Author George MacDonald Fraser, in his excellent book *The Hollywood History of the World*, says the film "was rated the height of daring and vulgarity at the time…cleavages having to be discreetly reshot for the American market." It was the first British movie to suffer changes because of the

PCA. Oddly, they were more concerned with the costuming than the morals of the title character. Despite the fact that she was a thief, murderess, and adulteress, the film was given a passing certification and released in the United States by Universal in December 1946.

Now the quest for an actress for the role of Amber St. Clare became the biggest casting call since David O. Selznick had searched for Scarlett O'Hara. Hollywood gossip columns wrongly suggested that author Kathleen Winsor was being considered to play the part of the tempestuous heroine she had created. Among the number of actresses who made early tests was a highly unlikely Tallulah Bankhead. Susan Hayward, who would become a Fox contract player in 1949, also tested for the part and was, for a time, considered a "likely candidate." Maureen O'Hara tested and wanted the part very badly, but she was only considered for the part of Bruce's wife Corinna. Angela Lansbury had read the book and felt she would be perfect as Amber, but at the time she was under contract to MGM. She begged Louis B. Mayer to suggest her to Zanuck, but the MGM mogul wasn't interested in pushing her for the part. Ms. Lansbury then went over his head and approached Fox herself through her agent. One biography of Angela Lansbury states: "She fervently believed that her being cast as Amber would allow her entry into the front ranks of movie stars." Although she was never seriously in the running for Amber, Fox did consider her for the role of the Countess of Castlemaine.

On the front page of the September 25, 1945, issue of *Daily Variety* there appeared a brief article entitled "Peggy Cummins From Britain Joins 20th." It said: "Peggy Cummins, 19-year-old British stage and screen actress, arrived yesterday from London for 20th-Fox term contract. She is cast opposite Peter Lawford in Ernst Lubitsch production 'Cluny Brown' which co-stars Jennifer Jones and Charles Boyer." Peggy was accompanied to Hollywood by her mother, Margaret. While Peggy was preparing for the role of "Betty Cream" in *Cluny Brown*, Darryl Zanuck decided she should test for Amber. For the test she was directed by John Stahl and dressed in one of Joan Fontaine's gowns from Paramount's *Frenchman's Creek* (1944), another film set in the Restoration period. The test was so impressive that Peggy was pulled from *Cluny Brown* and replaced by Helen Walker.

In October 1945, the same *Hollywood Reporter* article which had announced that John Stahl would be directing *Forever Amber* also stated that newcomer Peggy Cummins was the leading contender for the title role. In a pre-Story Conference memo issued to Philip Dunne and William Perlberg shortly thereafter, Zanuck said, "Please let us have no discussions about the lady who is to play <u>Amber</u>. For obvious reasons we don't want to mention it at this time." In the memo Zanuck does not refrain from making other casting suggestions. He mentions Lee J. Cobb as Almsbury ("If he can affect a convincing English accent"), Rex Harrison as Bruce ("I think he is the best Bruce Carlton in the world"), Victor McLaglen as Black Jack ("If he doesn't look too old"), Reginald

Peggy Cummins in her Forever Amber *screen test.*

Gardiner as King Charles II, Vincent Price as Rex Morgan, and Jessica Tandy as Nan.

According to studio records, the first person actually signed to appear in *Forever Amber* was Ralph Faulkner. Although his December 1, 1945, contract lists him merely as "actor," Faulkner was a fencing master who often played uncredited bit parts in "swashbucklers" in which he choreo-

Cornel Wilde and Ralph Faulkner.

graphed the fight scenes. Set to play a Cavalier in the early scenes, he would also be teaching swordsmanship to the other actors. For this his fee would be a mere $200.

Apparently loath to give up all the publicity being garnered by the search for Amber, Zanuck continued to test actresses. In all, 213 women were eventually tested for the part. On January 12, 1946, it was officially announced that Peggy Cummins had been chosen to enact the role. *Time* said: "Peggy Cummins, long the leader in the Hollywood clamber for the Amber role in *Forever Amber* — Irish born, London developed, 5 ft. 1 in., blond, baby faced, ripe-mouthed, grave-eyed and 20 — bagged it." Although Darryl Zanuck may have considered Rex Harrison "the best Bruce Carlton in the world," his appeal was as yet unproven with American audiences plus he was already committed to *Anna and the King of Siam*. Instead, Fox's handsome and temperamental contract player Cornel

Wilde was taken off suspension and given the part of Bruce. Wilde had just scored a tremendous success on loan out to Columbia playing Chopin in *A Song to Remember* (1945), which had gained him a large fan following in addition to a rather swelled head. Other members of the cast confirmed at this time were Vincent Price as Harry Almsbury, Glenn Langan as Rex Morgan, Reginald Gardiner as King Charles II, and Jessica Tandy as

Rene Hubert and Peggy Cummins.

Nan Britton. Filming was set to begin in March with a proposed budget of $3,000,000.

The selection of Peggy Cummins as Amber may have solved one of Darryl Zanuck's biggest problems regarding the film, but it created a new one for costume designer Rene Hubert. Hubert has already designed Amber's costumes, anticipating a more voluptuous actress than the diminutive Ms. Cummins, so he was forced to redesign her entire wardrobe.

Sixty-five costumes were designed for her and more than a dozen different workrooms throughout Los Angeles were utilized to make them, as the Fox wardrobe department lacked the adequate space needed. A total of $65,000 was spent to create Peggy Cummins' wardrobe as Amber.

Wardrobe problems aside, the casting of Peggy Cummins was greeted with enthusiasm from most quarters. Cinematographer Leon Shamroy was particularly effusive after photographing her early tests, "There is one of the most capable and sensitive actresses I've ever centered in the lens. She's got everything: imagination, scope, and the power of personality projection on the screen." However, with her angelic countenance, it would take considerable acting ability to portray the wanton vixen depicted in the novel. Ms. Cummins appeared unfazed: "I'm really not at all perturbed at the prospect of playing Amber. I think that an accomplished actress should be willing to tackle anything." But the pressures of the part were stacking up to be formidable. A March 10 *New York Times* article stated that of the 318 major scenes in the film, Peggy Cummins would appear in all but one. Except for one half day, she would be working continuously throughout the 92-day estimated shooting schedule. Director John Stahl added further pressure by saying that every day she missed would cost the studio $23,000. Making his new star feel at ease was apparently not of prime concern to Stahl. On March 4, Phyllis Adair was hired as an "understudy for Amber" at a rate of $200 per week.

With the major roles already cast, it was now time to concentrate on the supporting players. On March 8, 1946, Fox announced that the following actors had joined the cast: Peter Whitney as Black Jack Mallard, Eily Malyon as Mrs. Cleggat, Ian Wolfe as Matthew Goodegroome, Norma Varden and Lloyd Corrigan as Mr. and Mrs. Poterell, Paul Guilfoyle and John Rogers as members of Black Jack's gang, and Ethel Griffies as Mother Red Cap. Five days later, Aubrey Mather was signed for the part of Moss Gumble, the landlord at the Saracen's Head Inn. At that same time, John Meredith, who had appeared for director John Stahl in *Immortal Sergeant* (1943), was cast as one of Bruce Carlton's fellow Cavaliers.

In the meantime, a second-unit crew was sent to California's Montery Peninsula to photograph some of the few exteriors planned for the movie. It had been decided that, because of a major Influenza outbreak in Los Angeles, sets would be constructed on soundstages to represent the exterior scenes so as not to expose the cast and crew to any inclement weather and potential illness brought on by night shooting. With the anticipated cost of filming *Forever Amber* being so high, every precaution was to be taken to prevent any delays in production.

The daily shooting schedule lists the official starting date of production "A-491" as March 12, 1946. Principal photography actually began on March 13 with Amber observing Bruce Carlton and his band of Cavaliers riding into the village of Marygreen. The first week of filming was concerned mainly with scenes involving Amber and the Cavaliers at the Golden Lion Inn. The shooting went smoothly and, after viewing

Cornel Wilde and Peggy Cummins on the first day of shooting.

the rushes, studio executives were enthusiastic about Peggy Cummins' performance. Also during that first week of filming, more additions to the cast were announced: Margo Woode as Beck Marshall, Mari Aldon as Bess Columbine, and Sara Allgood, who replaced Ethel Griffies, as Mother Red Cap.

Filming continued on a six-days-a-week schedule, with only Sundays off. During the second week of shooting, the sequences in Marygreen were completed and work began on scenes set in London at the Saracen's Head Inn. These continued into the following week as well. On Thursday March 28, the scene at the Magistrate's Bench when Amber is sentenced to Newgate Prison was shot. The following day the production was shut down because Peggy Cummins had come down with the flu. Monday April 1, *Daily Variety* reported, "'Amber' on Vacation" due to the illness of the star. Two days later *Daily Variety* said "'Amber' Ambles Again" as Peggy was back to work and the filming had resumed. By now Amber St. Clare had been incarcerated in Newgate Prison and an unforeseen problem arose. For a scene to be filmed on April 4, seventy-six people were employed to impersonate prisoners in the Tap Room at Newgate Prison. Sixteen of them walked off the set because their makeup included the application of "lamp black and fuller's earth." Maintaining that this was not told them prior to their reporting for work, they appealed to the Screen Actors Guild, who denied their claim to be paid $16.50 each for reporting to the set that day.

The same day as the Newgate prisoner walkout, Natalie Draper signed her contract to appear in *Forever Amber*. The contract stated that she would play either Beck Marshall or the Countess of Castlemaine, which suggests that even though Margo Woode had already been signed to play Beck, a final decision had not yet been made. Ms. Draper had been an MGM contract player since 1943 and, although she appeared in eleven films, she had yet to receive a screen credit. Her most notable role thus far had been as one of the Vargas "Calendar Girls" in *DuBarry Was a Lady* (1943). Her *Forever Amber* contract included a clause which stated that she would be paid an additional weeks salary to dye her blonde hair to "suit our requirements." According to a Fox studio press release, Natalie Draper was the twenty-seventh actress to test for the part of Castlemaine. On April 9, *Daily Variety* announced that she had been added to the cast. The article did not specify what role she would be playing other than to say it "calls for a fist and hair pulling fight with Peggy Cummins," which sounds more like Beck than Castlemaine.

Throughout the production, Joseph Breen kept a watchful eye on *For-ever Amber*. Costume test stills for all the actresses who were to appear in the movie were regularly submitted to the PCA for approval and summarily rejected if the necklines were felt to be too low. Likewise any traditional songs from the period that might be used in the film had to be submitted for approval lest they contain any "offensive" lyrics. When

Costume test of Natalie Draper as the Countess of Castlemaine.

Forever Amber had been filming for about a month, Breen was asked to view the footage that had been shot thus far. In a memo dated April 19 to Colonel Jason Joy, Breen said, "This material appears to be generally acceptable under the provisions of the production code." However, he did go on to make some suggestions regarding fade outs on embraces and kisses. The same day as Breen's memo, the last major addition to the cast was made when Richard Haydn was assigned to play the Earl of Radclyffe, Amber's aged and cruel husband.

As filming progressed the pressures on Peggy Cummins continued to grow. Again, these were intensified by director John Stahl, who is reported to have openly complained that "she looks like a little girl dressed up in her mother's clothes." This understandably created resentment between the actress and her director, causing both to walk off the set on several occasions. In a January 1995 letter from Ms. Cummins she said, "I was certainly not happy doing it and began to lose a lot of weight." Toward the end of April, the scenes involving Amber at the Theatre Royal were filmed and it became all too obvious that no amount of makeup could give Peggy Cummins the more mature countenance she needed for the remainder of the picture. One movie magazine reported, "Nothing makeup experts could do to Peggy's exquisite skin and fragile features — without venturing into the grotesque — could make her look more worldly and mature before her time."

An April 29 *Daily Variety* article entitled "'Amber' Put to Bed for Week" said that the production was shut down again because Peggy Cummins had suffered a recurrence of the flu. The next day *Daily Variety* reported, "Stahl Out; 'Amber' to be Reshot." The article goes on to say that the filming had been halted on the pretext that Peggy Cummins was ill and that Stahl had been taken off the picture "because he had been 'riding' various members of the cast." Henry King and Joseph Mankiewicz are mentioned as the most likely replacements for director. The article concludes by saying, "Peggy Cummins expressed 'amazement' at the turn of events."

On May 1 the *Citizen News* ran an article announcing that production on *Forever Amber* has been postponed until late summer. Darryl Zanuck said, "The footage so far shot fails to measure up to the high standard of quality originally planned. We will have to review this footage and determine afterwards what changes, if any, will be made when the production is resumed." The article also says that director John M. Stahl had bowed out, but no other changes were anticipated and the cast would likely remain the same. The May 2 issue of *Daily Variety* ran the headline "Skouras in for 'Amber'." This article stated that Fox President Spyros Skouras had returned from a trip to England to deal with the crisis. Darryl Zanuck is quoted: "When production resumes, William Perlberg will continue as producer, and the present script by Philip Dunne will be used. No decision has yet been reached as to who will direct, nor have any changes in cast as yet been decided upon." However, the article did say that the film would now be likely shot in England and that Peggy Cummins was due

Peggy Cummins and director John M. Stahl.

to be replaced in the star role. Cummins was unavailable for comment, but her mother, Margaret, said: "We are both very weary over the whole matter. Peggy's plans are rather uncertain at present. From now on, it is up to her agent and the studio. I would like so much to say more but the studio has admonished us against making any statement."

Although there were certainly a number of factors involved, most of the blame for the shutdown eventually fell on Peggy Cummins' shoulders. A fan magazine article at the time said she was "plagued by constant exhaustion, worry over the picture, and by occasional digestive upsets." Her age seemed to be the main reason, while opinions of her acting ability were divided. Darryl Zanuck said, "We realized that Peggy could act the role, but she could never look it. She was too young." In a 1980 interview with Ronald L. Davis, Cornel Wilde said that the "dreadful, stupid script" was "old-fashioned, old-hat, pompous, static." Wilde said of Peggy Cummins: "She was a cute little blonde girl, who later became a very good actress. At that point little Peggy was very young, under Zanuck's wing. I mean to have her shoved into that tremendous role, inexperienced, not ready at all, was ridiculous. Zanuck finally admitted she just couldn't do it." In an April 1987 letter Philip Dunne wrote that Peggy Cummins was "Not up to it," but also placed blame on John Stahl saying, "He was hopelessly old-fashioned for my modern (then) script." Vincent Price also wrote in April 1987 saying that Peggy was replaced simply because "She looked too young" adding, "Miss Cummins would have been perfect — Linda [Darnell] was wrong for it."

Given her fine performances in other movies, Peggy Cummins acting was most likely not the problem. In stills from the early sequences of the scuttled version of *Forever Amber*, up to and including the scenes at Newgate Prison and Whitefriars, she looks perfect in the part. In later scenes, as the more sophisticated Amber, her innocent looks definitely work against her. In photos of her as an actress at the Theatre Royal, she looks out of place, overly made up, and very juvenile. Obviously, John Stahl was another major factor, as was the ever-problematic screenplay, but in the ensuing years, Peggy Cummins would become the scapegoat. *Forever Amber* had been shooting for 38 days and had cost the studio $1,880,647. Nearly two thirds of the original estimated budget had been spent, and Fox had nothing to show for it.

Shortly after Zanuck's announcement to stop the filming, Richard Haydn sent a letter to producer William Perlberg. Haydn began the letter by saying, "I want you to know how sorry I am about the headaches you have had with 'Amber.'" Haydn, who had been scheduled to begin filming around May 21, goes on to magnanimously relinquish his claim on the money owed him according to his contract ($3000) for participation in the first version of *Forever Amber*. This was an unheard-of gesture. He ends the letter by saying, "When later in the year, you start production again and if you still want me for 'Radclyffe,' I shall enjoy doing my best for you with that 'impotent old Earl.'" The role was such a change of pace for Haydn that he was extremely anxious to play it.

On May 5, 1946, the *New York Times* ran an article entitled "Next to Godliness is *Forever Amber*." The article states that Henry C. Link of the Psychological Institute of New York and Harry Arthur Hopf of the Hopf Institute of Management in New York had conducted a reading survey between December 1944 and May 1945. The survey showed that the novel *Forever Amber* ran a close second to the Bible in U.S. popularity. 95% of the people surveyed had read the Bible and 84% had read *Forever Amber*. This article was dutifully passed on to Joseph Breen at the PCA. His comments on this were not recorded.

CHAPTER FIVE

Reconstruction
of the
First Version

CAST OF ORIGINAL VERSION

Amber St. Clare	Peggy Cummins
Bruce Carlton	Cornel Wilde
Lord Harry Almsbury	Vincent Price
Black Jack Mallard	Peter Whitney
Capt. Rex Morgan	Glenn Langan
Earl of Radclyffe	Richard Haydn
Nan Britton	Jessica Tandy
King Charles II	Reginald Gardiner

"At Marygreen"

Matt Goodegroome	Ian Wolfe
Tom Poterell	Lloyd Corrigan
Mrs. Poterell	Norma Varden
Cavaliers	John Meredith, Ralph Faulkner

"At Newgate"

Mrs. Cleggat	Eily Malyon
Dead-Eye	Clyde Cook
Baliff	Harry Wilson
Moll Turner	Sandra Poloway

"At Whitefriars"

Mother Red Cap	Sara Allgood
Bess Columbine	Mari Aldon
Jimmy the Mouth	Paul Guilfoyle
Blueskin	John Rogers

And With

Beck Marshall	Margo Woode
Big John	William "Wee Willie" Davis
Moss Gumble	Aubrey Mather
Countess of Castlemaine	Natalie Draper
Mrs. Chiverton	Maureen Roden-Ryan
Dutchman	Sig Ruman
Coach Driver	David Thursby

Kay Riley and Marjorie Eaton were also hired for unspecified roles.

EXTANT PHOTOS TAKEN DURING THE MAKING OF THE UNFINISHED version of *Forever Amber* indicate that the sequences described below were completed. These do not always adhere to the proposed shooting schedule *(see Appendix 2, page XX)*. The quotes are bits of dialogue from the many early drafts of the script which never made it into the final version of the film.

Bruce Carlton and his band of Royalist Cavaliers ride into the village of Marygreen and seek rest and refreshment at the Golden Lion Inn.

Hoping to meet the Cavaliers, Amber goes to the innkeepers, Mr. and Mrs. Poterell, and offers to help serve their guests.

Amber: "Soldiers?"
Mrs. Poterell: "No — King's men. Cavaliers. The first I've seen in nigh fifteen years."

One of the men, Harry Almsbury, kisses Amber, but she is attracted to their leader, Bruce Carlton. She attempts to convince him to take her along when they depart for London.

> *Amber:* "I've never been to London. It must be wonderful."
> *Bruce:* "Why have you got such an itch to see London?"
> *Amber:* "Because I'll be killed if I stay here! The men of this village are sworn to take revenge on all who helped the king's return."

The next morning Amber waits by the side of the road and Bruce reluctantly agrees to let her go with them.

Bruce: "If I provide you with escort to London, it is with the understanding that I am not responsible for you — now — or at any time — no matter what happens."

Bruce, Almsbury, and Amber take lodgings at the Saracen's Head Inn in London. Bruce and Almsbury see Amber for the first time dressed like a lady of quality.

Bruce: "You're all the dreams of a fair woman a man ever had."

But Bruce is called away suddenly to Whitehall. When he returns, he tells Amber that he will be leaving soon on a privateering venture.

The next morning Amber awakens to the song of a bird sitting on the window sill. Looking around the room, she discovers that Bruce has already made his departure.

Amber, pregnant with Bruce's child, is sent to Newgate Prison for debt. She is put in a holding cell with drunken slattern Moll Turner, a Quakeress, and Nan Britton.

Mrs. Cleggat: "Good evening, ladies. I'm Mrs. Cleggat, wife of the jailor. As ladies of refinement, you'd understandably prefer more comfortable quarters. I can provide them for a consideration."

Amber and Nan are taken to the prison Tap Room where two of the prisoners fight each other over Amber. The fight is broken up by Black Jack Mallard, a highwayman.

> *Black Jack:* "You're new to our college, Madame? I must apologize for the scum that infests the place these days."

Black Jack offers Amber his protection if she will agree to be his mistress and go with him when he escapes prison.

Black Jack: "A dimber wench like you wasn't born to rot in prison. Though you'd best be warned, at that. 'Tis a merry life — but apt to be a short one."

Amber agrees to the bargain.

Black Jack: "A handshake means little in the outside — but you're dealing with thieves now. 'Tis your heart's oath — and mine."

Amber goes into labor the night of the planned escape with Nan by her side.

Black Jack takes Amber and Nan to a thieves' den in Whitefriars run by Mother Red Cap. Amber gives her baby up into the keeping of a country woman.

Amber: "You'll let me know at once if he falls sick, Mrs. Chiverton?"

Bess Columbine, Black Jack's former mistress, is jealous of Amber and picks a fight with Jack over her.

Bess: "D'ye think I'll stand back and watch you throw yourself away on a milk-faced nanny goat like her?"

Black Jack devises a plan for his gang to rob a coach, using Amber as bait.

> *Black Jack:* "Here's the lay. A king's coach leaves the city at three tomorrow, carrying army pay for the coast garrisons."

Mother Red Cap is skeptical and angry that Black Jack is attempting to take matters into his own hands without her consent.

> *Red Cap:* "When you're ready to do the thinking for this band, let me know and we'll examine your qualifications!"

Amber stands by the crossroads and pretends to be a lady in distress.

Amber: "We've lost a wheel — and my men need help to replace it."

When the coach stops to help her, Black Jack and his men come out of hiding with pistols drawn.

When the coach robbery fails and Black Jack is killed, Amber seeks refuge with Almsbury at the Saracen's Head Inn.

    Amber: "Have you heard word from <u>him</u>?"
    Almsbury: "'Tis senseless. You may never see him again. There's little chance he'll ever return to Marygreen."
    Amber: "I'm not going back there. I tell you I'm not going back. I'll wait for him here."

Almsbury uses his influence to get Amber a job as an actress. Backstage at the Theatre Royal, Beck Marshall, one of the other actresses, is jealous of all the attention paid to Amber.

Beck: "Look here, Mistress What-d'ye-call, you needn't strut like a crow in the gutter. The gentlemen will have a swing at anything new."

Amber: "'Tis some years since they troubled you, I take it?"

Captain Rex Morgan arrives backstage at the theatre and encounters Amber.

Rex: "Your pardon, Madame. I'm calling on Mistress Beck Marshall."

In the Theatre Royal Tiring Room, Amber walks in on Nan and Big John who voice their concerns about the plague.

> *Big John:* "They say a gold piece is sovereign against the sickness."
> *Amber:* "Rot. Are you a pair of babies? I never saw such a taking."
> *Nan:* "Please, m'lady, we shouldn't be staying here. All the gentry are leaving. M'lady — think of the little boy!"
> *Amber:* "Very well — you may take Bruce to Mistress Chiverton's — and your big lout of a sweetheart, too."

The scenes were being filmed in mostly chronological order of the script and after the Theatre Royal sequences, shooting was halted. At this point it becomes very noticeable that Peggy Cummins looks too young to play the part of an older and more sophisticated Amber. Otherwise, Zanuck's concern about maintaining a "high standard of quality" seems to have been unfounded in regard to the production itself. Physically, it looks magnificent, with beautiful costumes and atmospheric sets. It also seems to be very appropriately cast. All the scenes which are supposed to be exteriors have obviously been filmed on soundstages, in keeping with the misguided intention of "protecting" the cast and crew from the flu, but this is not a detraction by any means and only adds to the atmosphere.

Although Cornel Wilde once said that Zanuck had the negative and prints burned so nobody could see "what a horrible mistake he had made," footage from the scuttled version of *Forever Amber* was stored at Technicolor in Hollywood for years, but now it is apparently lost forever.

CHAPTER SIX

A Brief Intermission

IN LATE APRIL 1946, WHILE THE FIRST VERSION OF *FOREVER Amber* was still in production, Darryl F. Zanuck invited Otto Preminger to spend the weekend at his house in Palm Springs. Agent Charles Feldman was also invited this particular weekend. Feldman was the agent for both Preminger and John M. Stahl. The day after he arrived, Preminger was approached by Zanuck and Feldman to discuss *Forever Amber*. Zanuck said that Stahl was doing a "terrible job" and that he was going to take him off the picture. He wanted Preminger to take over saying, "I have arranged for you to see all the film shot so far. Monday you will tell me what you want to do." Preminger replied, "I'll tell you now what I want to do. I want not to do *Forever Amber*. I read the book when it was sent around by the story department. I found it terrible." Zanuck reminded Preminger that he was "a member of the team" and must accept the assignment. Zanuck's choice of Otto Preminger was not an idle one. Preminger had taken over the direction of *Laura* from Rouben Mamoulian and had turned a potential disaster into one of the studio's biggest hits.

The following week, Preminger viewed the existing *Forever Amber* footage and thought Peggy Cummins' performance was "amateurish" and that the script was "appalling." He went to Zanuck and consented to do the film if he could have a two- or three-month delay in order to have a new script written and choose another actress for the lead. Zanuck agreed to Preminger's demands and shortly thereafter stopped production on *Forever Amber*. Curiously, in the early announcements of the film's shutdown, Preminger was not even mentioned as a candidate for director.

In June, Otto Preminger was officially announced as the new director. In a July 14, 1946, article in the *New York Times*, Preminger would not discuss why the production was halted other than to say "somehow all the elements didn't jell." He also said that he would "tell the story of 'Amber' without making it a peep show or violating good taste." The same article mentioned that Gene Tierney might be a replacement for the title role but that "she's not set and other people are under consideration." Ms. Tierney's husband Oleg Cassini urged her to pursue the part but in her autobiography she said, "I disliked what I heard of the script and thought the story was trash."

In Oleg Cassini's autobiography, *In My Own Fashion*, he relates a different story: "The trouble was, Gene was [Zanuck's] second choice and she knew it. Zanuck was in a spot; if Gene played her cards right, she could have negotiated anything out of him at that point. But she was too proud. She refused to take the part, even though Zanuck eventually offered annuities worth several million dollars if she'd accepted. I thought she was crazy."

Otto Preminger's first consideration was a new script. He brought in writer Ring Lardner, Jr., who had won an Academy Award for *Woman of the Year* (1942). Lardner had also stepped in and accomplished successful rewrites on the scripts of *The Cross of Lorraine* (1943) and *Cloak and Dagger* (1946). Zanuck asked Philip Dunne to stay on the project and collaborate with Lardner. Dunne later said, "Ring shared my contempt for the material, and we worked well together." According to Dunne, the script was rewritten about 40% but he still felt that "there is simply no way to overcome the handicap of having chosen the wrong subject matter in the first place."

Meanwhile, Otto Preminger had decided that Lana Turner would be perfect for the part of Amber. Although she was under contract to MGM, Preminger was sure that Louis B. Mayer would loan her out for a picture as high profile as *Forever Amber*. Zanuck refused, not wanting to give such a career-boosting opportunity to someone who was not under contract to Fox. Preminger was determined and gave a dinner party to which he invited both Lana Turner and Zanuck. In Preminger's biography he says, "She flirted shamelessly with Zanuck, at one point even sitting on his lap. But he would not change his mind." Ms. Turner was also having an affair with Fox's biggest star Tyrone Power. This was causing no end of headaches for Fox and MGM. Power was not yet divorced from his wife Annabella at the time and both studios were trying to avoid any bad publicity. And the production of *Forever Amber* certainly did not need any further controversy attached to it. Although Darryl Zanuck may have had several good reasons for not wanting Lana Turner, the main one was that he had already made the decision of who would play Amber when filming resumed.

Lana Turner costume test for The Three Musketeers.

CHAPTER SEVEN

Enter
Linda Darnell

when she signed her contract with 20th Century-Fox on April 6, 1939, and became "Linda Darnell." A remarkable dark-haired beauty, by her third picture, *Star Dust* (1940), she was already a star with her name above the title. She appeared, often cast opposite Tyrone Power, in a series of "good girl" parts in such films as *Daytime Wife* (1939), *The Mark of Zorro* (1940) and *Blood and Sand* (1941).

Linda shocked both her family and Darryl F. Zanuck when she eloped to Las Vegas with Fox cameraman J. Peverell ("Pev") Marley in April 1943. Linda was nineteen and Pev Marley was forty-two. Zanuck, who insisted that she had damaged her screen image, retaliated by firing Marley and suspending Linda. Although public opinion was on Linda's side, she continued to be punished by Zanuck, who persisted in casting her in a series of minor parts. A loan out to United Artists for *Summer Storm* (1944) proved to be a turning point in her career. In this adaptation of Chekhov's story, "The Shooting Party," she was cast against type as a sensuous bad girl. Zanuck responded to her new image and the rave notices she had received by giving her more diverse roles in better pictures. One of these was as an avaricious waitress in *Fallen Angel* (1945) for director Otto Preminger. Both the film and her performance were received with considerable enthusiasm by audiences and critics alike.

In early 1946 two of the most ambitious productions in Fox's history were in the planning stages, *Captain from Castile* and *Forever Amber*. As one of the studio's most beautiful and popular leading ladies, Linda Darnell hoped to be considered for the role of Amber, but Zanuck had already decided she would play "Catana" in *Captain from Castile* opposite her frequent co-star Tyrone Power. While *Captain from Castile* was in pre-production, Linda appeared in three more films. One of these was *Centennial Summer* (1946), again under the direction of Otto Preminger. Working on this picture Linda felt her leading man Cornel Wilde was aloof and that Preminger was tyrannical. She looked forward to appearing in *Captain from Castile* as she had pleasant past working relationships with both Tyrone Power and director Henry King.

Shortly after the search for an actress to play Amber was first announced, *Silver Screen*, one of the popular fan magazines of the time, ran an article suggesting that Linda would fit the bill perfectly. They even featured a photo of Linda in which they retouched her hair to show how she would look as a blonde. But, as far as the studio was concerned, at that time she wasn't even being considered. In the meantime, Linda signed her contract to play "Catana" and began to prepare for the role.

When filming on *Forever Amber* was stopped, it was the talk of Hollywood. At the time Darryl Zanuck was quoted as saying, "I have said we had trouble making 'Forever Amber.' That is putting it mildly. We had spent two years in research for the perfection of the production but we also wanted perfection in the casting." Now Zanuck had come to the conclusion that Linda Darnell would be the "perfect" Amber. When she was told of his decision, she regretted giving up *Captain from Castile* (Catana would be played by newcomer Jean Peters), but realized that the part of Amber could well be the role of a lifetime. Years later she said, "I was practically living and breathing Catana when I got word that I was to play the new Amber. Naturally it was the most thrilling surprise that has ever come to me. I thought I was the luckiest girl in Hollywood." Her enthusiasm was only slightly dampened by the fact that she would again be working with Otto Preminger.

On July 25, 1946, columnist Hedda Hopper announced, "Linda Darnell got the green light yesterday for the role of Amber." With rehearsals scheduled to begin on the September 4, Linda had just over a month to prepare for the part. First on the agenda was to change her dark brunette hair to blonde. It took seven bleachings by hairstylist Gladys Witten to get the correct shade required for the Technicolor cameras. Rene Hubert was now able to use his original costume designs as Linda possessed the type of figure he had in mind when he originally planned Amber's wardrobe. Forty-two costumes were made at a cost of $90,000, which was $25,000 more than the total spent on costumes for Peggy Cummins. A Fox press release said: "Rene Hubert designed his costumes exactly as clothes were made during the Restoration era. Each dress averaged 20 yards of material. Each gown had the bodice rigidly boned and laced up the back in the manner of the times. The gowns averaged 35 pounds; one weighed 58. An average of ten people worked on each outfit." By comparison, Clinton Sandeen created the entire men's wardrobe at a total cost of $125,000.

British actress Constance Collier was hired as a dialogue coach for Linda, to give her manner of speech an English cadence, without attempting to affect a British accent. Actor Alan Napier (later "Alfred" on the *Batman* television series) had previously been hired for a similar task as "dialogue director" on the Philip Dunne script of February 22, 1946. Now that the "right" actress had been found to play Amber, the rest of the cast had to be considered. Cornel Wilde, Glenn Langan, Natalie Draper, and Jessica Tandy were retained from the first version. Ms. Tandy was the only player who had been mentioned as far back as Zanuck's first memo regarding casting suggestions. Vincent Price was on loan-out filming *The Long Night* at

Costume test of Linda Darnell as Amber.

R.K.O. and was no longer available to play Almsbury so the part was given to Richard Greene. Greene was delighted to be cast in such an important production. This would be his first film in Hollywood since returning from England following the War and, as such, would be instrumental in reacquainting him with the American movie-going public. The other important roles recast were John Russell as Black Jack and Anne Revere as Mother Red Cap. George Sanders had read the novel and wired William Perlberg and Otto Preminger asking that he be considered for the part of King Charles II. Both agreed that he would be perfect and Sanders was signed on.

On July 31, Philip Dunne and Ring Lardner Jr. turned in a Shooting Final. This script reinstates a 1644 prologue, which gets the story off to an exciting start. The characters of Mrs. Cleggat and Big John are eliminated. The Earl of Radclyffe's Italian man-servant, "Galeazzo," is added. The screenplay ends with an exchange of dialogue between Amber and Nan concerning Sir Thomas Dudley (a character not in the original novel). Darryl Zanuck returned the script to the writers with a handwritten note on the first page: "Examine episode by episode. Needs editing badly — too long at 'Red Caps' — too long at theater with Morgan — find short cut. Are you prepared to cut?"

Rehearsals began, as scheduled, on September 4 and continued for over a month. On September 26, British actress Margot Grahame was added to the cast in the role of Bess Columbine. Otto Preminger had already decided that he would take a more realistic approach to the material than his predecessor had done. He insisted on more authenticity in the sets and the costumes. He also intended to use far more exterior shooting to eliminate the "set bound" look of the first version. The production tied up ten of the Fox sound stages. It encompassed an 18 acre set of the city of London, 22 exteriors, and 102 interiors. Leon Shamroy returned as cinematographer on the film. Discussing *Forever Amber* in his autobiography Preminger said, "One redeeming factor was that I met Leon Shamroy on that picture, a brilliant cameraman and a marvelous friend." In the book *Hollywood Cameraman: Sources of Light*, Leon Shamroy discusses his approach to making the film: "In *Forever Amber* I matched the title by using Amber-coloured gelatins. I shot all the exteriors, or many of them, in actual rain. I wanted a dull, monotonous effect, and I used liquid smoke hovering over the bodies when they painted the doors red to indicate the presence of plague." Shamroy also employed the use of "the ultimate lamp," the new Type 450 lamp which could project an intense beam of light over long distances. Recalling his participation in *Forever Amber* in 1987, actor John Russell made specific mention of "Leon Shamroy's fabulous cinematography."

On October 10, Dunne and Lardner turned in a Revised Shooting Final and once again, Alan Napier was hired to peruse the script in his capacity of "dialogue director." On October 22, William Perlberg happily honored his obligation to Richard Haydn and recast him as the Earl of Radclyffe. Two days later, on October 24, *Forever Amber* (now known as production "A-504") went before the cameras for a second time. The first

Linda Darnell as she appears in her first scene in Forever Amber.

scene to be filmed took place in the Goodegroome kitchen where Amber refuses to marry Bob Starling. The same day that *Forever Amber* resumed filming, Darryl Zanuck sent a memo to William Perlberg, Philip Dunne, and Ring Lardner Jr. regarding the script of October 10. The memo begins, "Here is the only point I have left to talk about on the script of *Forever Amber.*" Zanuck goes on to request a more "emotional and dramatic reaction" from Amber after Radclyffe has informed her of Bruce's departure following the plague sequence. Zanuck ends by saying: "Otherwise, as I have said earlier, it is a wonderful script in every respect." Ring Lardner Jr. revised this scene to Zanuck's specifications and submitted it to him on October 31.

As it came time to begin filming Cornel Wilde's scenes, the actor attempted to quit the production and was again placed on suspension. The studio claimed that he had quit because he wanted a salary increase.

Wilde said his reasons for leaving were that he disliked the film, didn't want to work with Preminger, and needed a vacation. The dispute was settled two days later when his salary was increased to $200,000 for forty weeks work per year, making him the third highest paid actor at Fox. In his 1980 interview with Ronald L. Davis, Wilde said, "I didn't want to be in it, didn't want to work with Otto again. I felt that Otto

Otto Preminger and Linda Darnell.

would make a heavy, ponderous film, which didn't turn out to be the case. He made a very good film." Unfortunately, Otto Preminger didn't agree and in later years considered it to be the worst picture he ever made.

On November 7, the Screen Writers Guild held an arbitration to determine the writing credits for *Forever Amber*. The official decision was that the credits should read as follows:

> *Screenplay by Philip Dunne and Ring Lardner, Jr.*
> *Adaptation by Jerome Cady*
> *From the novel by Kathleen Winsor*

As with Peggy Cummins before her, Linda Darnell soon began to feel the immense pressures of the role of Amber. Linda knew that Preminger had protested when she was cast in the lead and she felt that he was "holding her back in the part." Linda's sister Undeen later said, "[Linda] was not one to dislike many people but Preminger she couldn't tolerate. He was a good director, but a mean SOB. She hated him." Linda and her husband Pev Marley had separated shortly before her involvement with *Forever Amber* and this, coupled with Otto Preminger's unsympathetic treatment of her were beginning to affect her physically as well as emotionally.

Despite this Linda gave her all as Amber. Cornel Wilde said of her: "Everybody liked Linda. I mean she was a nice girl. The crew all loved her, always pleasant and considerate and sweet. She was secure in her acting. She was not a top caliber actress, I don't think she had that, but she was a capable actress. In *Forever Amber* I think she gave a really good performance."

Linda worked six days a week often from 4:30 in the morning until 8:00 at night. On November 11, she was sent home from the set with a fever. It had been planned that the following Sunday 138 members of the cast and crew would go to the Monterey peninsula for a week of location filming. Linda was diagnosed as having mastoiditis, the result of an acute middle ear infection, and was off the picture for a week while she recovered. When Linda was considered fit enough to travel, she took the train to Monterey accompanied by a nurse. There she joined the rest of the cast and crew at the Del Monte Lodge. The plans were to film a coach robbery sequence and a sword fight between Cornel Wilde and Glenn Langan. Unfortunately, Margot Grahame came down with pneumonia and had to be hospitalized. Since she played an instrumental part in the coach robbery it was difficult to shoot the scene around her. Preminger decided to film the scenes scheduled for Monterey back in Los Angeles instead. This trip had cost the studio an estimated $100,000 with only some publicity shots of Linda in Monterey to show for it. The majority of the exteriors were filmed on the extensive Fox backlot, sometimes utilizing refurbished European sets originally built for *The Song of Bernadette*. Other Los Angeles location shooting was done at the Rivera and Hillcrest Country Clubs and Bush Gardens.

Linda Darnell had always suffered from weight problems and it was felt by her doctor that constant dieting was contributing to her increasingly rundown condition. On the set, she would now be under the constant supervision of a nurse. Back at Fox, shooting resumed on November 30 and Linda began filming the scenes at Mother Red Cap's thieves den in Whitefriars with Margot Grahame, John Russell, and Anne Revere. The following scene was filmed on December 4, but it would eventually be cut from the final film:

> *Bess:* "Who's she?"
> *Black Jack:* "A likely wench I found in Newgate. You'll be teaching her our trade."
> *Bess:* "I'll teach her to keep out of places she isn't wanted!"

> She advances on Amber, but Black Jack catches her.

> *Black Jack:* "Now then, Bess, let's have no trouble. There's room for all here."
> *Bess:* "Not for me and her! Not in the same house!"

> She grabs Amber by the shoulders and shakes her violently.

The following day the elaborate coach robbery sequence in which Bess betrays Black Jack and Amber was filmed. By the end of that week all of the principal scenes involving Margot Grahame as Bess had been completed.

Preminger now prepared to film the sword fight sequence between Cornel Wilde and Glenn Langan which was to take place in a fog-shrouded field at dawn. Preminger and Leon Shamroy tried dry ice to get the fog effect, but it didn't last long enough. Cornel Wilde said that they eventually utilized an oil mixture called Nujol which was used in laxative medicines. It produced the required effect but turned the grass to slim. At one point during the duel, Glenn Langan slipped on the slick grass and his sword narrowly missed slicing Cornel Wilde's head. The Nujol also gave many of the members of the cast and crew diarrhea from breathing it.

Although George Sanders had lobbied to appear in the film, once filming began he did not appear to be very engaged in the production. According to Cornel Wilde, Sanders spent most of his time sleeping on the set and only roused himself when absolutely necessary. In Richard Vanderbeets' biography, *George Sanders: An Exhausted Life*, Wilde relates the following story: "George and I were sitting at a table, and the cameraman was lighting us. George fell sound asleep. When the lighting was ready and the director called for a rehearsal, I said my first line and then switched to my imitation of George and said his first speech. He awoke to hear himself acting." The crew was amused, but Sanders was not.

One of the most complicated, and costly, sequences in the film was the Great Fire of London. After weeks of preparation, the scene was shot in January 1947 on the Fox lot at three in the morning with fire trucks standing by and traffic blocked off for a mile around the studio. Despite some concern by nearby residents, who thought it was a real fire, the scene was completed successfully. Linda Darnell suffered a minor burn when a

Glenn Langan and Cornel Wilde.

roof caved in, but this was the only mishap. Although they were separated, Pev Marley had continued to be a source of constant emotional support for Linda throughout the filming. Pev and Linda had spent much of the Christmas and New Year holidays together. Three weeks into the New Year the couple announced their reconciliation. Linda moved back into their home and they began plans to adopt a baby.

On January 28, 1947, Macmillan Company wrote a letter to Fox: "As you probably know, early in March there are to be hearings in the Massachusetts court in connection with the book *Forever Amber*. We understand our opponents are going to prove that the motion picture has been dropped because it was just too 'hot' for a movie." The publishers requested that Fox provide letters to the contrary. Fox responded on February 6 with the following statement: "Please be advised that under the date of October 24, 1946 we commenced principal photography of our said motion picture *Forever Amber*. We anticipate that the principal photography of the motion picture will be completed around the middle of March 1947. *Forever Amber* should be released in the United States around the end of the present calendar year." Macmillan was fighting against the "New England Watch and Ward Society," those watchdogs

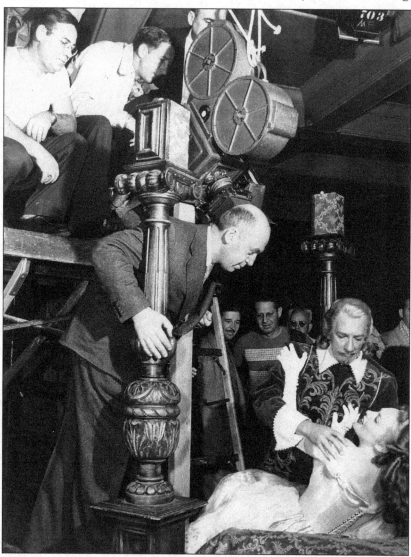

Otto Preminger directs Richard Haydn and Linda Darnell.

of morality who had initiated the banning of the novel in Boston. The Massachusetts court eventually decided in favor of Macmillan Company saying that the book "while conductive to sleep, is not conductive to the desire to sleep with a member of the opposite sex."

In a February 9 *New York Times* article, "Green Light for 'Amber,'" Otto Preminger said that after fifteen weeks of shooting he was "prepared to predict that the picture will not be remade again. The censors, the studio's executives, and even the technical advisors appear to be satisfied with the material shot." The original shooting schedule had called for the final week of principal photography to be completed on January 9. Unforeseen delays and frequent script revisions had already extended the proposed shoot beyond the original 99 days estimate. In his autobiography Preminger said, "It went on and on, the longest shooting schedule I ever had." Three days before the end of filming, Linda Darnell collapsed on the set and was sent home. A few days later she returned to complete the final scene, the ball at Whitehall Palace, and principal photography officially ended on March 11, 1947.

After viewing the existing footage, Zanuck called a for story conference on April 2 with William Perlberg, Otto Preminger, Philip Dunne, and Ring Lardner Jr. Zanuck suggested that a scene be added in Amber's bedroom following her refusal to marry Bob Starling. This sequence would help to establish her character early in the film. He also wanted to revise and simplify the death of Black Jack and have Amber seek refuge with Rex Morgan. He requested a "retake" of the scene where Amber takes leave of Little Bruce, allowing him to go to America with his father. Adding scenes in a dressmaker's shop was also discussed. Zanuck proposed that the following scene between Nan and Little Bruce at Amber's wedding to Radclyffe should be eliminated from the film:

> *Little Bruce: (excitedly)* "They're going to come out now! Mother's coming out!"
> *Nan: (reprovingly)* "No, Bruce — remember. Who's coming out?"
> *Little Bruce: (correcting himself)* "Madame."
> *Nan:* "And who is your mother?"
> *Little Bruce:* "You are. *(then, rebelling)* Why can't she still be my mother and be a countess, too?"

It was decided that once the new material had been written, *Forever Amber* would go back into production for two weeks to shoot the additional scenes requested by Zanuck.

On April 3, a lengthy revision of the scene in which Amber arrives at the Saracen's Head Inn was added. This is followed by another scene in which Almsbury and Bruce walk in on Amber taking a bath. Originally, Moss Gumble, the landlord of the inn, was supposed to steal the money that Bruce leaves Amber upon his departure from London. Now three new scenes were added which introduce two characters not found in the novel: the dressmaker Mrs. Abbott and her friend Mr. Landale. It is they who swindle Amber out of her money and cause her to be sent to Newgate Prison. Norma Varden, who had played Mrs. Poterell in the first version of *Forever Amber*, was hired to play Mrs. Abbott. Alan Napier, who was a "dialogue director" on both versions, was to play Mr. Landale. Also submitted on April 3 was the scene in which the Earl of Radclyffe consoles Amber following the death of Rex Morgan.

Dunne and Lardner offered a new sequence on April 7 which would replace the coach robbery. Now Amber and Black Jack attempt to rob a drunken fop in the London streets. Black Jack is shot down by the Watchmen and Amber flees. Going through an unlocked door she hides in the kitchen of Rex Morgan. When he discovers her presence there, she convinces him to protect her from the Watchmen. Also submitted on this date was a revision of the scene in which Amber gives her son over to Bruce. In the final film, excerpts from the original version of the scene and this revision are combined to even greater effect.

On April 8, the last new contribution was made to the script. This scene, which takes place in Amber's bedroom in the Goodegroome cottage, turned out to be an important addition to the picture. It is played without dialogue and shows Amber in her room trying to imagine what she would look like as a "lady." She unwraps a bundle which contains a picture of ladies of the Court which has been torn from a book, a necklace, and a fragment of mirror. This sequence establishes her yearnings to become a great lady and creates sympathy for the situation in which she finds herself. It also helps to justify her adverse reaction to marrying Bob Starling.

Filming resumed on April 7 and continued through April 24. The last scene shot was between Amber and Radclyffe following the death of Rex Morgan. Darryl Zanuck now viewed the finished film and decided that it ran too long. He felt that the optimal running time for a film of this type should be no more than two hours and thirty minutes. He later said: "Since the beginning of the motion picture industry, I do not believe that there have been more than twenty-five pictures which have run more than two hours and a half. And these included some of the big epics." The running times for such Fox epics as *Captain from Castile*, *The Robe*, and *The Egyptian* exemplify his bias. Regarding *Forever Amber*, Zanuck still felt that too much time was spent in the Mother Red Cap section of the story. With the coach robbery already eliminated, it was a simple task to remove all the remaining scenes featuring the character or Bess. As of May 7, Margot Grahame's part had been entirely cut from the picture and she was no longer listed in the official studio credits.

In late May, *Forever Amber* was submitted to the PCA for approval. On May 27, Joseph Breen responded: "The finished picture is objectionable because it deals excessively in illicit sex and adultery. While it is true that these objections are treated deftly and without offensive details, by the same token they are made to appear attractive." Breen complained about three particular points:

1. *Amber's neglectful treatment of her child.*
2. *Bruce does not "pay" for his wrongful conduct.*
3. *Radclyffe's manservant kills him out of anger and vengeance.*

He also had several suggestions to make:

1. *The film should limit the illicit sex between Bruce and Amber to one incident, and that in London.*

2. *All illicit sex between Amber and any other male characters, except Charles II, should be removed.*

3. *Reinstate the "Voice of Morality" on the parts of Almsbury and Bruce.*

4. *Remove all social and financial assets gained by Amber.*

Most important — Strengthen bonds of affection between Amber and her son so her loss of him at the end will be appear greater.

Exception was taken to several specific scenes, which would need to be altered or cut to get full PCA approval. It was also noted that the finished film was 50% to 60% different from the script which had been approved by the PCA in November 1946. The film was returned to Fox on June 9 to be re-edited to the PCA's specifications. One of the scenes objected to involved an exchange between Amber and Beck Marshall

(Susan Blanchard) backstage at the Theatre Royal, which had been added to the script by Ring Lardner Jr. on January 7, 1947.

> *Fop:* "Upon my honor, Mistress St. Clare, you look more beautiful every performance."
> *Amber:* Thank you, sir.
> *Beck:* You waste your time, Sir Walter. She's the property of an officer in his Majesty's Guards, aren't you, dear?"
> *Amber: (sweetly)* It's better than belonging to a whole regiment, Mistress Marshall."

The elimination of this scene reduced Susan Blanchard's part to little more than a wordless extra.

Of all the scenes which were excised prior to the film's release, perhaps none is more sorely missed than the first love scene between Amber and Bruce which takes place in the forest outside the Golden Lion Inn. In the final film, Amber returns to the inn after everyone has gone to sleep. She awakens Bruce and attempts to convince him to take her to London with him. The scene fades out after Bruce kisses her and she walks out of the tavern. As originally filmed, the sequence continues with Bruce following Amber into the forest where he finds her sitting by a stream. There is an exchange of dialogue where they discuss the stars and Amber attempts to turn the conversation once again to London. Bruce refuses to discuss the subject.

Feeling they have had enough of preliminaries, Bruce moves closer to her, his arm slipping around her.

> *Bruce:* "What's your name?"
> *Amber:* "Amber."
> *Bruce:* "Amber? A strange name."
> *Amber:* "I always wondered what it meant. Then last year a clerk from Cambridge stayed the night at our inn. He told me." (She turns to look at him. Their faces are very close together.)
> *Amber:* "It's the stuff they use in making jewelry — smooth — and when you hold it to the light — it shines like gold. And here's magic in it — for if you stroke it, it gives out a blue fire..."

After this dialogue, the directions read: "His mouth comes down hard on hers; her head goes back over his arm." This scene obviously typified the "illicit sex" that the PCA was objecting to, but it is a pity that it had to be cut. The elimination of intimate exchanges like this damages the relationship of the characters toward each other. Scenes such as this also give the story some "breathing room" and a sense of pacing which would have been a respite from the fast clip at which the plot often unfolds. Because of the PCA's demands, much of the "romance" in this romance is missing.

There were many publicity shots in magazines of Amber in a bathtub

Bruce and Amber in the deleted first love scene

at the Saracen's Head Inn. When the scene was cut, a variety of reasons (none of them referring to censorship) were given. A studio publicity release made the following excuse: "Amber's bathtub scene was cut out of the picture when researchers pointed out that people in the time of King Charles II didn't bathe. They used perfume instead." Of course, this is utter nonsense. *Life Magazine* said the scene was cut out "because the producers felt too many recent movies had bathing scenes." Surprisingly, this scene was not mentioned in the list of suggested cuts from the PCA, although from the content it certainly seems like something that would have caused them consternation.

Knowing Bruce is out; Almsbury deliberately walks in on Amber while she is taking a bath:

Amber: (furiously) "Get out!"

Almsbury: "Now, sweetheart — there's no reason to be angry."

Amber: "You'd better be careful. His lordship might return."

Almsbury: "Bruce? What of it?"

Amber: "He'd run you through!"

Almsbury: "Don't fret about my welfare, sweet. Or rather, do. My most crying lack at the moment is a kiss."

Amber in deleted bath scene.

He bends down to her. Amber splashes a stream of soapy water into his face and he retreats. The door opens and Bruce comes in, taking in the scene with a look of astonishment.

Bruce sends Almsbury away and Amber "melts into his arms" as "he kisses her." Considering that Zanuck had vetoed a bathtub scene written for the Peggy Cummins version, it is surprising that he ever approved the inclusion of this as one of the additional sequences to be filmed.

A change in dialogue was requested by the PCA in a scene where Amber asks Rex Morgan for five pounds. He replies: "But I gave you five pounds two weeks ago. And I've paid the rent." The PCA insisted that "And I've paid the rent" be deleted. During the scene in Mrs. Chiverton's country cottage, where Amber has taken Bruce to meet his son for the first time, Bruce says "I've enjoyed these few days here." The line was changed to "I've enjoyed this day" so it would not imply that he and Amber had spent any nights together. At the end of this scene, "With a quick gesture, [Amber] pulls his face down to hers and they go into a passionate kiss." The scene was altered so that it fades out as they move toward each other. The next shot shows Bruce and Amber returning to the lodgings she shares with Rex in London. The PCA suggested that this scene be darkened so it would look like the evening of the same day they left for the country but this change was never made. A few weeks later, Fox returned the re-edited and re-dubbed offending reels to the PCA. On June 20, 1947, the organization finally gave *Forever Amber* a formal seal of approval (certificate #11495) confirming that the film was now in an acceptable state for release. In addition to this, Joseph Breen sent a lengthy memo to Eric Johnson, president of the Motion Picture Association of America, explaining his reasons for passing the picture.

The shooting estimate for the second version of *Forever Amber* had been 99 days. It actually filmed for 112 days, plus 17 days for the additional scenes and retakes. The estimated budget for the second version had been $3,684,000, but it had ended up costing $4,494,453. This, added to the money spent on the scuttled version, came to a grand total of $6,375,100, making *Forever Amber* the most expensive movie of its day. Darryl F. Zanuck still felt that he had a potential gold mine in the film, although he did not foresee additional problems which were looming on the horizon.

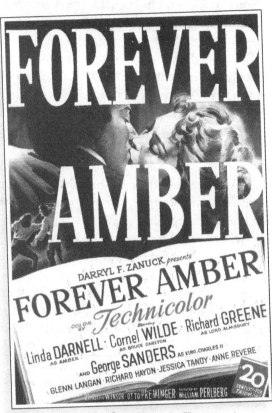

One Sheet for Forever Amber.

CHAPTER EIGHT

The Movie
... At Last!

Official Studio Credits

Darryl F. Zanuck *presents*

FOREVER AMBER

Directed by . . . . .Otto Preminger
Produced by. . . . . .William Perlberg
Screenplay by. . . . . .Philip Dunne and Ring Lardner, Jr.
Adaptation by . . . . Jerome Cady
From the Novel by. . . . . .Kathleen Winsor

Color by Technicolor

Technicolor Director. . . . . Natalie Kalmus
Associate . . . . Richard Mueller

Music by. . . . . David Raksin
Conducted by. . . . . Alfred Newman
Orchestral Arrangements . . . . . . Maurice de Packh and Herbert Spencer
Director of Photography . . . . .Leon Shamroy
Art Direction. . . . . .Lyle Wheeler
Set Decorations . . . . .Thomas Little and Walter M. Scott
Film Editor. . . . . Louis Loeffler
Wardrobe Direction . . . . Charles Le Maire
Costumes Designed by . . . . Rene Hubert
Hair Stylist. . . . . Irene Brooks
Makeup Artist. . . . . Ben Nye
Special Photographic Effects . . . . Fred Sersen
Sound . . . . Alfred Bruzlin and Harry M. Leonard

Uncredited Technical Advisors
Godfrey Davies, Fred Cavens, Nick S. Trani, Harry Mendoza

Cast

Amber St. Clare. . . . . Linda Darnell
Bruce Carlton . . . . Cornel Wilde
Lord Harry Almsbury . . . . .Richard Greene
King Charles II . . . . .George Sanders
Capt. Rex Morgan. . . . . .Glenn Langan
Earl of Radclyffe . . . . Richard Haydn

Nan Britton . . . . Jessica Tandy
Mother Red Cap . . . . Anne Revere
Black Jack Mallard . . . . John Russell
Corinna Carlton . . . . Jane Ball
Sir Thomas Dudley . . . . Robert Coote
Matt Goodegroome . . . . .Leo G. Carroll
Countess of Castlemaine. . . . . .Natalie Draper
Mrs. Spong . . . . Margaret Wycherly
Lady Redmond . . . . Alma Kruger
Lord Redmond . . . . Edmond Breon
Landale . . . . .Alan Napier

Other cast members not listed in the official studio credits include,
in order of appearance:

Sarah Goodegroome . . . . Edith Evanson
Bob Starling . . . . .Richard Bailey
Mr. Starling . . . . Houseley Stevenson
Tom Poterell . . . . Alan Edmiston
Mrs. Poterell . . . . Betty Fairfax
Jack, a wounded cavalier . . . . Marten Lamont
Moss Gumble. . . . . .Arthur Gould-Porter
Mrs. Abbott. . . . . .Norma Varden
Tybalt. . . . . .Ian Keith
Magistrate . . . . .Robert Greig
Baliff . . . . .David Thursby
Quaker Woman . . . . Victoria Horne
Marge. . . . . .Ellen Corby
Turnkey . . . . Tom Dillon
Dead-Eye . . . . Will Stanton
Blueskin . . . . .Skelton Knaggs
Midwife. . . . . Tempe Pigott
Drunken Fop. . . . . .David Ralston
Ivers. . . . . .Tom Huntley
Killigrew . . . . .Tom Moore
Beck Marshall. . . . . Susan Blanchard
Mrs. Chiverton . . . . .Ottola Nesmith
Little Bruce (age 3) . . . . .Jimmy Lagano
Galaezzo. . . . . Jimmy Ames
Queen Catherine . . . . .Lillian Molieri

Little Bruce . . . . .Perry "Bill" Ward
Makeup Artist . . . . Pati Behrs

"AMBER...THE WOMAN...THE PICTURE... YOU'LL REMEMBER — FOREVER!"

BY THE TIME *FOREVER AMBER* MADE IT INTO MOVIE THEATERS, the story had been drastically altered. The end result is significantly different from the novel, the original Jerome Cady screen treatment, and the Philip Dunne scripts for the unfinished version. In all there were nine different versions of the script. Here, in brief, is the final film narrative as originally released.

> *1644 — "The English Parliament and Oliver Cromwell's army have revolted against the tyranny of a corrupt monarchy. England is aflame with civil war..."*

A Royalist coach is being pursued by Cromwell's Roundhead soldiers. The coach stops at a farmhouse. The passenger jumps out, puts a bundle on the doorstep, and knocks on the door. The farmer, Matt Goodegroome (Leo G. Carroll), comes outside just in time to see the soldiers overtake the coach, killing the occupant and the driver. Goodegroome picks up the bundle and sees that it is a baby. He calls his wife Sarah (Edith Evanson) and they both notice that the blanket wrapped around the child has the name "Amber" embroidered on it.

> *1660 — "Oliver Cromwell is dead. The House of Stuart, in the person of Charles II, has been restored to the throne of England. But though London acclaims the restoration of the monarchy, in the small towns and villages the tradition of the Puritans still runs deep and strong..."*

The story resumes in the village of Marygreen, where Amber (Linda Darnell) has grown up as the adopted daughter of Matt and Sarah Goodegroome. At dinner one night, Matt announces his plans for her to marry Bob Starling (Richard Bailey), the son of another farmer. Amber refuses and he sends her to her room as punishment. A band of Royalist Cavaliers arrives at the Goodegroome cottage asking for food and lodging. Matt sends them off to the Golden Lion Inn as Amber watches from the window of her room. Amber sneaks out and goes to the Golden Lion where she offers to help the innkeeper and his wife serve their guests. Amber is immediately taken with the leader of the Cavaliers, Bruce Carlton (Cornel Wilde). She waits until everyone else has gone to sleep and then approaches him about taking her with them to London. He refuses, but he is obviously attracted to her. They kiss and Amber leaves the tavern.

London: Bruce and his fellow Cavalier, Harry Almsbury (Richard

Matt and Sarah Goodegroome with the orphaned baby Amber.

Greene), arrive at Whitehall Palace with the hope of seeing King Charles II (George Sanders) and collecting recompense owed them for serving him in the war. Sir Thomas Dudley (Robert Coote), the king's equerry, refuses admittance saying that Charles is too busy to see them. He is not too busy to see his latest mistress Barbara Palmer (Natalie Draper), who sweeps past them through the door without even waiting to be announced.

Bruce and Almsbury return to the Saracen's Head Inn, where they have taken lodgings, to discover that Amber has followed them to London. Bruce agrees to let her stay until he can obtain finance from the king for a privateering venture. Although Almsbury warns Amber that Bruce will never marry her, she falls even deeper in love with him. When Bruce attempts to renew an old acquaintance with Barbara Palmer, a jealous King Charles finances Bruce's sea voyage to be rid of him. Bruce departs

London without telling Amber, but leaves her two hundred pounds res-titution. Amber goes to her dressmaker, Mrs. Abbott (Norma Varden), to pay money owed. Mrs. Abbott and her accomplice Mr. Landale (Alan Napier) swindle Amber out of all her money and then testify against her when she is sent to the Magistrate (Robert Greig) on a charge of debt. Amber is found guilty and committed to Newgate Prison.

Amber serves the Cavaliers.

While in prison, Amber is befriended by Nan Britton (Jessica Tandy) and accompanies her to the Newgate Tap Room. There, Amber attracts the attention of the infamous highwayman, Black Jack Mallard (John Russell). Black Jack offers to take Amber with him when he escapes, in return for her favors. She agrees, because she is carrying Bruce's child and does not want it to be born in prison. Black Jack and Amber escape the night she goes into labor. He takes her to his hideout in Whitefriars which is run by the greedy Mother Red Cap (Anne Revere). Amber gives birth to a son, whom she names Bruce. When she has recovered, Mother Red Cap sends her out with Black Jack and his gang to rob the rich fops who frequent the London taverns. During one such robbery, Black Jack is shot and killed by the night watchmen and Amber is forced to flee to escape arrest. In her efforts to get away, Amber goes through the unlocked door of a nearby building and finds herself in a pantry. It is the home of

Capt. Rex Morgan (Glenn Langan), an officer in His Majesty's Guards. When Rex discovers her hiding there, she begs him not to turn her over to the watchmen. He is immediately attracted to her and offers her his protection. Rex uses his influence to obtain her a job at the Theatre Royal knowing that actors are wards of the Crown and immune from arrest.

Amber is now an actress at the Theatre Royal and living with Rex

Black Jack and Amber strike a bargain.

Morgan at the Plume of Feathers Inn with Nan Britton as her maid-servant. On stage she attracts the attention of both the elderly Earl of Radclyffe (Richard Haydn) and King Charles himself. Although Rex is in love with Amber and wants to marry her, she cannot forget Bruce. When Bruce returns to London, Harry Almsbury brings him backstage to see Amber. Since Rex is on a mission in Wales, Amber decides to take Bruce to the country home of Mrs. Chiverton (Ottola Nesmith), who has been caring for their child. Bruce is enchanted by the boy and tells Amber he would consider staying in England as a farmer, but he will not return to life at Court. When they return to Amber's lodgings in London, Rex has come back unexpectedly. Mad with jealously, he challenges Bruce to a duel. The next morning the duel is fought and Rex is killed. Bruce is filled with remorse over the unhappiness that both he and Amber have caused and he walks out on her.

While Amber is in mourning for Rex, the Earl of Radclyffe calls to offer his condolences. He makes it obvious that he wants to marry her. Amber agrees to marry him in order to become "Countess of Radclyffe," with the hope that her new title will impress Bruce. Amber's wedding takes place at the Radclyffe country estate while in London the plague is spreading. Almsbury attends the wedding and at the reception he tells

Jealous Rex Morgan is hopelessly in love with Amber.

Amber that Bruce is in London overseeing the unloading of his ships. Amber imprudently deserts her new husband and drives a horse and cart to London to find Bruce. Amber locates him at the docks and soon realizes that he is suffering symptoms of the plague. She takes him to a deserted house in order to care for him. A district nurse, Mrs. Spong (Margaret Wycherly), is sent to help care for Bruce. Instead, she tries

Amber fights the evil Mrs. Spong to save the life of Bruce.

to kill him in order to steal his gold watch. Amber catches her in the attempt and the two women fight. Amber kills her in self-defense. Bruce develops a "plague boil" and after Amber lances it, he begins to recover. One day, while Amber is out marketing, the Earl of Radclyffe arrives at the house and informs a surprised Bruce that Amber is his wife. Bruce departs and when Amber returns, Radclyffe tells her that she will never see Bruce again.

After months of seclusion at Radclyffe Manor, Amber and Radclyffe are summoned to attend a ball at Whitehall Palace. Once again, Amber attracts the attention of King Charles who dances with her and then asks that she join him for supper. The jealous Radclyffe insists that they leave the ball immediately. They return to Radclyffe Manor as a great fire sweeps out of control through London. When Radclyffe thwarts Amber's attempt to return to Whitehall, they have a violent argument.

He locks her in her room as the house begins to burn around them. Nan and Radclyffe's man-servant Galeazzo (Jimmy Ames) come to Amber's rescue and Radclyffe is left to die in the flames.

Several months have passed and Amber has supplanted the Countess of Castlemaine (the former Barbara Palmer) as King Charles' favorite. She now lives in Whitehall with Little Bruce (Perry Ward) and Nan. One

Radclyffe threatens Amber.

afternoon, Amber and Charles are strolling in St. James Park. They unexpectedly meet Bruce Carlton who has recently returned to London from America with his new wife Corinna (Jane Ball). A few days later, Bruce calls on Amber. She hopes that it is to renew their romance, but instead he asks permission for him and his wife to adopt Little Bruce and take him to their home in Virginia. Amber refuses and insultingly questions the virtue of Corinna. Bruce asks Amber to reconsider his request and then takes his leave. Angry and disappointed, Amber concocts a scheme to prove to Bruce that Corinna is no more virtuous than she is. Amber sends an invitation to Lady Carlton to attend a private supper with herself and King Charles at Whitehall that evening.

At supper, Amber's forced gaiety cannot compete with Corinna's reserved charm. Afterwards, pleading a headache, Amber leaves Charles and Corinna alone in what is an obviously compromising situation. She

Amber, King Charles, and Corinna have supper.

Amber gives Little Bruce to his father.

rushes back to her rooms to send a message to Bruce telling him of his wife's infidelity with the king. Charles walks in on her unexpectedly and tells Amber that, realizing he was being used as "pawn in a dirty game," he has sent Corinna home. Amber attempts to convince him of her innocence, but Charles' pride has been injured. He insists that she leave Whitehall for good the next day.

The following morning a tearful Amber is overseeing the packing of her belongings when she is visited by Sir Thomas Dudley. Sir Thomas invites her to supper and tells her that it isn't necessary for her to leave so quickly. Amber is indignant at his suggestion, but her anger is cut short by the arrival of Bruce. Bruce is about to depart for America and once again asks Amber let him take his son. Amber tells Bruce that she will let their son decide and is devastated when Little Bruce chooses to go with his father.

Amber watches from her window as Bruce and her son walk out of her life forever.

She turns away and calls to Nan, instructing her to inform Sir Thomas that she will accept his invitation to supper.

CHAPTER NINE

A Holy Crusade

prepare for the release of their most anticipated, and most expensive, production. The first public showing of *Forever Amber* was at a sneak preview on October 3, 1947, in Morgantown, Ohio. A week later, *Daily Variety* ran an article entitled "'Amber,' 'Castile' Usher Out Big Coin Spectacles." It said that *Forever Amber* and *Captain from Castile* were, for the time being, the last of the big budget costumers coming out of Hollywood. Fox had cancelled their plans to film Thomas B. Costain's *The Black Rose* because it would "run well into the multi-million production brackets." This was to have been Cornel Wilde's follow-up film to *Forever Amber*. (It was eventually made by Fox in 1950 with Tyrone Power.)

On October 15, Fox upped their order of 400 Technicolor prints of *Forever Amber* to 475. The studio had already lined up 3,102 advanced priced roadshow play dates between October 22 and December 29. This included 80 key theaters in Canada. Fox estimated that by the middle of December, every U.S. city with a population of 10,000 or more would have played the picture. Immediately after New Years, an additional 1,520 play dates had been set. The advanced price release would charge 80 cents for matinee tickets and prices ranging from $1.20 to $1.80 for evening performances.

The official world premiere of *Forever Amber* was held in New York's Roxy Theater on October 22, 1947. Accompanying the film was a "Gala Stage Review" starring Yeloz and Yolanda, and Sid Caesar. The first day's gross was $23,000, which topped all previous Roxy records. *Daily Variety* said, "Three hundred years ago, the beaux stood in line for 'Amber.' They did it again today." On October 24, *Daily Variety* reported that *Forever Amber* had grossed $48,000, the all-time high for the first two days of any attraction at the Roxy.

Although the Catholic Church had failed in their attempts to prevent the production of a movie version of *Forever Amber*, now that the film was in release they redoubled their efforts against its exhibition. The day of the New York premiere, the Catholic Legion of Decency placed the movie on their "Condemned" list. The Legion said, "This film in the nature of the story it tells and the manner in which the behavior of the central characters is presented constitutes glorification of immorality and licentiousness." Leading the pack in the Church's holy crusade was Francis Joseph Cardinal Spellman, Archbishop of New York. Cardinal Spellman declared that "Catholics may not see *Forever Amber* with a safe conscience" and this message was read at all Sunday masses throughout the country.

The Catholic Legion of Decency had been established in 1934 and enjoined all Catholics, under pain of mortal sin, from seeing the films it condemned. Once a year, all Catholic congregations were called upon to take the "Legion of Decency Pledge." The same day that *Daily Variety* announced that *Forever Amber* was setting a two-day house record at the Roxy, they also ran an article with the heading "Bishop Bans Film." The article concerned a Catholic Bishop in Fall River, Massachusetts, who asked the local exhibiter not to show *Forever Amber* in his theater. When he refused, the Church took out an ad in the local paper condemning the film. At the same time, a Police Chief in Providence, Rhode Island, took it upon himself to ban the film in that city. The following day, Fox president Spyros Skouras issued a counter statement saying, "I must disagree very firmly with and protest as unfair and harsh the position taken by the Legion of Decency. I am compelled to state that I believe it has erred in taking an extreme stand in this instance and that the final verdict must come from the public."

In the meantime, the movie continued to rake in the dough. After five days *Forever Amber* had taken in $140,000 at the Roxy and by the end of the first week the total had reached a record $180,589. Roxy manager A.J. Balaban called it "unquestionably the greatest weekly figure ever compiled by any attraction in any theater anywhere." A typical *Daily Variety* headline said: "'Amber' Setting Record at Roxy, Tops B'way B.O." *Forever Amber* opened in Los Angeles on October 29 and set an all-time record one-day gross of $24, 250 in six theaters. The October 30 *Daily Variety* ran a front page article, "'Amber' Bow Here Sets B.O. Mark." It listed the following grosses for the six theaters showing *Forever Amber*:

Lowe's State	$10,000
Grauman's Chinese	$4,400
Fox Uptown	$3,400
Loyola	$2,350
Westwood Village	$2,100
Beverly	$2,000

In that same issue of *Daily Variety*, Fox took out a full page ad with the banner: "Yesterday 'Forever Amber' smashed all opening day records in 26 theaters in Greater Los Angeles... keeping pace with new grosses 'Amber' is setting throughout the nation." During its opening day on the West Coast, *Forever Amber* played 80 theaters in Southern and Northern California and took in $164,427. This issue of Daily *Variety* also reported, "Amber Glow on B'way Continues."

Determined to protect their parishioners from moral decay, the Catholic men's organization, The Archdiocesan Union of Holy Name Societies, publicly declared *Forever Amber* to be "unwholesome entertainment." The City Commission in Grand Rapids, Michigan, banned the film in their city on "moral grounds." Thankfully, not all city officials were so easily swayed. In a March 30, 1999, article in the Mobile, Alabama, newspaper *The Harbinger*, dealing with film censorship in Mobile during the 20th Century, author R. Bruce Brasell wrote: "In October 1947, the chief of

Holy Name Men in Philadelphia protest the showing of Forever Amber.

police viewed the first screening of *Forever Amber* along with representatives of the Mobile chapter of the Catholic based Legion of Decency organization. The police chief, much to the outrage of the local Bishop, declared the film violated no city ordinances."

On November 4, *Daily Variety* ran an article with the heading "Only 'Amber' Shows Glow Among Bleak Chi Boxoffices." It goes on to say that although current movie attendance was distressingly low in Chicago, *Forever Amber* had grossed a record-breaking $130,000 in its first two weeks at the State Lake Theater. Although the movie was performing well in many engagements, Avro Manhattan's 1949 book *The Vatican in World Politics* states that as a result of the Legion of Decency's "Condemned" rating some theater managers who had already booked the film were asking to be let out of their contracts. On November 7, the Allied States Association of Motion Picture Exhibitors informed Fox that "In addition to the Legion's condemnation of the subject, it appears that every Catholic Bishop is taking special action in his diocese. Thus we read of exhortations not to see the picture, of theaters being picketed, and of usherettes declining to work during the engagement of the film." Some Catholic Bishops threatened theater owners that they would not only boycott theaters during the engagement of *Forever Amber*, but up to a year afterwards if they did not immediately agree to stop showing the film. In Philadelphia, Archbishop Dennis Cardinal Dougherty demanded that theaters showing *Forever Amber* and Howard Hughes' *The Outlaw* withdraw the films within 48 hours. The theater managers responded by saying that the pictures would run as long as they were doing good business. Dougherty retaliated by sending members of The Holy Name Society to picket the offending theaters. Spurred on by the actions of the Catholic Church, local censors in thirty-six states also joined the campaign to prevent the showing of *Forever Amber*.

When the attendance for *Forever Amber* began to drop noticeably, Fox president Spyros Skouras was forced to "eat crow." He asked Otto Preminger to come with him to New York for a meeting with the Rev. Father Patrick J. Masterson, executive secretary of the National Legion of Decency, and two other priests. According to Preminger's autobiography, Skouras pleaded his case, but Father Masterson coolly informed him that the book had been banned so Fox should have known better than to make a movie out of it. At this point Preminger says that Skouras knelt before the priest, kissed his hand and begged, "Father, Father, please help!" Father Masterson said that they would consider removing it from the "Condemned" list if the title of the film were changed to disassociate it from the offending novel. Skouras rightly reasoned that without the title they really didn't have anything. He instructed Preminger to view the film with the priests and make any changes they requested. Father Masterson later informed the Catholic Tribunal that "We secured from Mr. Skouras his approval of actually making the cuts in prints of the picture." Spyros Skouras also had to publicly "apologize for earlier statements by Fox executives criticizing the Legion for condemning the picture." On December 5, 1947, Skouras issued the following statement: "I wish at this time to correct an unfortunate impression created by statements made by us incident to the disapproval of the original version of 'Forever Amber' by the Legion of Decency. These statements were interpreted as questioning the right of religious leaders to guide the adherents of their faith on moral questions. No such purpose was intended, neither was it our purpose to indicate any acceptance whatsoever of the theory that the popularity of a motion picture is a true criterion of its moral character."

Prints of *Forever Amber* were briefly withdrawn and the cuts were made. When the film went back into circulation, it had been cut from 140 minutes to 138, but those two lost minutes damaged it irreparably. A prologue (which Preminger claimed was written by Father Masterson himself) was spoken over the opening credits:

> *"This is the tragic story of Amber St. Clare, slave to ambition, stranger to virtue, fated to find the wealth and power she ruthlessly gained wither to ashes in the fire lit by passion and fed by defiance of the eternal command- the wages of sin is death."*

As if this weren't bad enough, the ending of the film was altered. In the original version Amber watches from a window as Bruce takes their son away. She closes the window and…

There is a short pause, then Amber, with eyes full of tears, speaks quietly:

Amber: "Nan."
Nan: "Yes, Amber."
Amber: "Tell Sir Thomas Dudley I'll be happy to have supper with him tonight."

Nan nods and goes out of scene. CAMERA MOVES WITH AMBER over to her dressing table and mirrors. She sits down and begins methodically to apply makeup to her face. As we move into a FULL CLOSE UP of her white, tragic image in the mirror. FADE OUT

The Catholic Church erroneously felt that this implied some kind of triumph on Amber's part so the scene was eliminated. Instead, as Amber

One of several kissing scenes which were cut from Forever Amber.

closes the window, we hear a voiceover from Bruce with dialogue from earlier in the film: "Haven't we caused enough unhappiness? May God have mercy on us both for our sins" …THE END.

These were the two major changes, but there were also a number of minor ones, including further fadeouts on kisses just before the lips were shown touching. One of the oddest changes of all was in a scene in which the Countess of Castlemaine berates King Charles for taking his queen to the ball at Whitehall: "I'm not going if you insist on bringing that Portuguese scarecrow!" The line was re-dubbed as: "I'm not going if you insist on bringing that petulant scarecrow!" With these changes made, the Catholic Church was now appeased and elevated the film to "Class B- Objectionable in Part for All" status. In *The Vatican in World Politics*, author Avro Manhattan addresses the *Forever Amber*/Legion of Decency issue and concludes: "Thus a great Film Corporation had to submit before a tribunal set up by the Catholic Church, sitting above the Courts of the United States of America, judging, condemning and dictating, not according to the laws of the country, but the tenets of a Church which, thanks to the power of its organizations, can impose its standards upon, and therefore indirectly influence, the non-Catholic population of the country."

Linda Darnell blonde again in The Walls of Jericho *with Kirk Douglas and Cornel Wilde.*

After being granted its "Class B" status, *Forever Amber* was returned to theaters and went on to become the fifth highest grossing film of 1947 in the United States after only having been in release for less than three months. The original "advanced admissions" release in the U.S. and Canada yielded a total take of $3,777,193. When the film went into its "popular priced" release, the total increased to $4,797,300. *Forever Amber* was released throughout the rest of the world the following year and it made another $3,064,000 in foreign rentals.

The studio had requested that Linda Darnell keep her hair blonde for the London premiere of *Forever Amber*, which had been postponed because of tax reasons. Her next film was *The Walls of Jericho*, once again with Cornel Wilde, and under the direction of John M. Stahl. For the second and last time in a film, Linda was blonde.

The *Walls of Jericho* was finished and in release by August 1948. The following month *Forever Amber* opened in London. Discussing the film in his *1948 Film Review*, British author Maurice Speed said: "*Forever Amber*, as we all rather expected, came as a promised 'bang' and went off like a damp squib." Philip Dunne, who remained resentful about being forced to work on the picture, said, "Linda Darnell was certainly better than Peggy Cummins, although the title carried the picture. It became a conversation piece. But *Forever Amber* was a national joke." In his book *Twentieth Century-Fox: A Corporate and Financial History*, author Aubrey Solomon says: "On the surface, with world rentals of $8 million, *Forever Amber* was considered a hit at distribution level. However, production overages led to a final negative cost of $6.3 million. With the additional expense of advertising, publicity, and distribution overhead the movie could never recoup its costs."

In the final analysis, the movie had become a qualified success. Although millions of dollars had been taken in, the costs had been high… in emotions, finances, and integrity. The content of the film had been compromised severely and the original uncut version was never to be shown publicly again.

CHAPTER TEN

Excerpts from Contemporary Reviews

Daily Variety — October 10, 1947

First thing to be said about *Forever Amber* is that it is the undisputed high-gloss glamour production of the year to date. And it isn't likely to be surpassed in that respect. Miss Darnell makes a thoroughly convincing and sympathetic Amber. It is a tribute to Miss Darnell's acting and Otto Preminger's direction that the part is kept entirely within the bounds of propriety without losing too much strength. In directing the piece, Preminger has exhibited high skill and alert control in putting across the sex elements of the yarn by suggestion and implication without weakening their appeal to audience interest.

Film Daily — October 10, 1947
Monumental production brilliantly produced, directed, and acted gives a sound honest return for every cent spent or asked.

Darryl Zanuck has done splendidly by "Amber." In the two hours and 20 minutes that it takes to tell the story there is created a motion picture of monumental stature. It is BIG in every interpretation of the word. Otto Preminger's direction is evident in a flowing, fluid continuity which aptly captures the essence of the novel. In this respect the multitude that read and re-read the book won't be disappointed. Selection of the cast was masterful. Linda Darnell in the title role is a vivid "Amber" and her beauty in Technicolor has breathtaking quality.

Hollywood Reporter — October 10, 1947
Striking, Colorful, Screen Adaptation

Forever Amber, a popular novel, has become a spectacular and colorful screen drama, designed to enjoy the same widespread success and, one might add, the same controversy which featured the appearance of the book. To be sure, the amorous courtesan has been considerably subdued in the interests of celluloid expediency, but nevertheless she remains beautiful, intriguing, and shocking. Linda Darnell in the title role is nothing short of superb, effecting the transition from country bumpkin to a woman of sophisticated assurance with the ease of the polished actress she has turned out to be. What is more, she reads sympathy into Amber which the character sorely needs.

Boxoffice — October 11, 1947 (J.M. Jerauld)
Film's "Amber" Retains Excitement of the Book

Otto Preminger, the director, and William Perlberg, the producer, have shrewdly kept the colorful characters in the foreground at all times. Linda Darnell gives a vivid portrayal of Amber. Some costume pictures on opulent backgrounds get lost in their settings. This never does. The story dominates throughout. What would have been censurable in the book has been handled so delicately that it is difficult to see how anyone can object to anything in it.

Motion Picture Herald — October 11, 1947 (Red Kann)

"Forever Amber," the sensation-packed novel by Kathleen Winsor, sold over 2,000,000 copies. "Forever Amber" the film, can never disavow its parentage, nor does it try. The answer is an attraction which lives up to the advance buildup created for it by 20th Century-Fox. Linda Darnell plays Amber, and does it surprisingly well. She is costumed magnificently and handled throughout with loving camera hands and eyes. That makes her something to behold.

Harrison's Reports — October 18, 1947

A great spectacle, magnificently produced and photographed superbly in subdued Technicolor. It should prove to be a record-breaking box-office attraction, for there is a ready-made audience of millions who, having either read the book or heard about its torrid tale, will be anxious to see it. And they will not be disappointed, for, although the story has its shortcomings, it holds one's interest throughout. As "Amber," Linda Darnell turns in a surprisingly good performance, and her beauty, enhanced by the rich and revealing costumes of the period, is easy on the eyes. All others in the cast turn in creditable performances, but none matches the superb playing of George Sanders, as Charles II, who walks off with every scene he appears in. The action moves along at a steady pace and at times is highly exciting.

Cue — October 25, 1947
"Forever Amber" in Technicolor Splash is Costume Saga of Lady of Many Loves

For all that this lavish, gaudy and flamboyant Technicolored drama of a Restoration adventuress and her twenty amours is reputed to have cost a thundering $5,000,000, there is less here than meets the eye. What does meet the eye is a fabulously luxurious production. As for the filmplay itself, the most that can be said for it is that the almost incessant sound and fury and dazzle on screen occasionally succeed in covering up the lamentable paucity of the story, its slick superficiality, and its dime-novel tawdry quality.

New Yorker — October 25, 1947

It would be hard to match the egregiousness of the novel *Forever Amber* in any medium…but the movies have made a try. The film, which has the same name, is tawdry, colorful, and gamy.

St. Petersburg Evening Independent — October 25, 1947
Much Cleaned Up "Forever Amber" Provides Splendid Entertainment

"Forever Amber," as a production, is up to Darryl Zanuck's standard, which is high. The widely heralded picture provided splendid entertainment, but movie-goers who expected as much bedroom atmosphere as they found in the Kathleen Winsor novel were disappointed. A good deal of cleaning up was done on the movie version. Linda Darnell makes a convincing Amber. Beautiful, ambitious and unscrupulous, she lets nothing stand in the way of her upward climb to position and wealth except her love for Bruce Carlton, played expertly by Cornel Wilde. It is a colorful, spectacular show which sustains interest.

New York Times — October 26, 1947 (Bosley Crowther)
Shading 'Amber'
A Very Famous Female is Dimmed in Her Debut

The Legion of Decency condemned it and Cardinal Spellman publicly proclaimed that no one of the Catholic faith could see it with a conscience completely safe. Such an austere reception for a picture — and especially one of "Amber's" hue — could only mean that its excesses were on a pretty elaborate scale. And that they are, beyond question — although it must be honestly said that they're nothing like as intimate and gaudy as they were in Miss Winsor's nursery tale. But Amber is still an obvious trollop, lusty and luxurious as Linda Darnell parades her in a wealthy wardrobe of brilliant gowns, and the singular substance of the story is Restoration wantonness.

Los Angeles Daily News — October 30, 1947 (Virginia Wright)

Forever Amber is not only amorously tame, as a piece of cinema fiction it is monumentally dull. Two such good screen writers as Philip Dunne and Ring Lardner Jr, with Jerome Cady who made the adaptation, are credited with this screen version, but apparently Miss Winsor's novel was beyond their powers of redemption. And because the writers couldn't seem to draw any spark of life from the story, composer David Raksin and conductor Alfred Newman must have felt compelled to make up in background noise what the action lacked in fervor.

Los Angeles Examiner — October 30, 1947 (Dorothy Manners)
'Amber' Film Excels Book

It's a big, gutsy, colorful and Technicolor-ful adventure story, constantly a delight to the eye and so tightly scripted and directed that it moves with the exhilaration of a small cyclone. [Linda Darnell] is a splendid and vivid Amber, performing with mature ease that tops anything else she has ever done on the screen. The direction and pace Otto Preminger gives the picture should certainly make him an "Oscar" candidate, and while it cannot be denied that William Perlberg had a "problem" child on his hands producing this picture, he should be proud and delighted that the result is smash screen entertainment.

Los Angeles Times — October 30, 1947 (Edwin Schallert)
'Amber' Rare Scenically; Dull in Plot

One has this ultimate feeling regarding *Forever Amber*, namely that it is one of the most artistically produced pictures scenically ever to arrive on the screen but that, simultaneously something approaching an appalling waste attends the using of all the lavish and beautiful film footage to surround a character that is scarcely interesting even as a trollop. The picture leaves a sense of emptiness that is far more hollow than brass and certainly much less reverberant than a tinkling cymbal.

Life — November 3, 1947
Deprived of beds, the famous trull seems merely dull.

Forever Amber, 1945's best-seller about the beauty who went from mattress to mattress across Restoration London, turned up as a movie last week. "You'll forever remember *Forever Amber*" was the publicity slogan under which customers fought past the box office, leering with anticipation. But what they saw was like a fallen soufflé. After the censors finished with Kathleen Winsor's heroine, she seemed more like a wanton teen-ager than the most famous pushover in recent literature. Many would wonder why Hollywood had bothered cleaning up a book whose only real strong point was vulgarity.

Time — November 3, 1947

Forever Amber (20th Century-Fox) is every bit as good a movie as it was a novel. But it may not be as sensationally popular as Kathleen Winsor's account of a Slut's Progress. Many who admired the book may be disappointed to learn that in the picture Amber is allowed only four of her numerous lovers. What's more, she gets an even crueler comeuppance, without (as far as the camera can see) having much fun earning it.

Look — November 25, 1947
Costly costume film cleans up the best-selling story of a bad girl.

Handsome sets and costumes, beautifully photographed in the best Technicolor to date, make the film a constant delight to the eye. Amber's rise from a provincial town to a palace involves less sex on the screen. The lovely heroine is now ambitious and amoral but never ruthless or blatantly sinful. Linda Darnell is a beautiful and able Amber. In the large supporting company, Richard Greene and George Sanders are especially good. Producer William Perlberg and Otto Preminger have turned a difficult story into an entertaining period piece.

Family Circle — January 1948

Surprise! Darryl Zanuck has actually done it! *Forever Amber* is a good motion picture by almost any standard, either on its own or as a condensation of Kathleen Winsor's galloping marathon. Linda Darnell isn't a great actress, but she has all of the beauty, some of the brains, and enough of the instincts to give Amber and audience a run for their money. Nearly two and a half hours of dazzling entertainment that is lusty without being bawdy and a distinct improvement on the best seller.

Christian Herald — 1948
Forever Amber
Definitely not recommended

As a courtesan who is neither convicted nor convincing, Linda Darnell will have a hard time living this one down. Its theme is inexcusable, and its action just plain dull. Even the morally weak who may be attracted by its buildup as a "condemned" feature will be disappointed as they are duped.

CHAPTER ELEVEN
Aftermath

AFTER THE ORIGINAL RUN, WHICH LASTED MORE THAN A YEAR, *Forever Amber* went out of release and was not seen again for several years. In 1953 it was reissued (in black and white!) as a "20th Century-Fox Encore Hit" and played in 2,615 theaters with a take of $94,000.

In December 1957, NTA Telefilm Associates acquired a package of Fox films to show on television. Included in this package was *Forever Amber*. Assuming that the original negative still retained "unacceptable material," NTA requested that Fox arrange for the negative in the possession of Technicolor to be cut according to the print approved by the Legion of Decency. Thus, there would be no problems with the television showings. On January 14, 1958, Fox responded to NTA saying that the negative at Technicolor has "already been edited to length of expurgated version."

During the following years, there were several attempts to mount a remake of *Forever Amber* but none of them came to fruition. In July 1959, director Robert Aldrich approached Fox in an attempt to secure rights to *Forever Amber* for a remake. A month later Fox responded by saying they were not interested in disposing of the rights at that time. No more was heard about a remake of *Forever Amber* until August 1976 when Mona Moore and Associates, a project development firm for motion pictures and television, inquired if Fox would sell the motion picture and television rights to *Forever Amber*. Once again Fox responded negatively. In April 1977, Henry Jaffe Enterprises, represented by Mona Moore and Associates, contacted Fox and expressed interest in developing a TV mini-series based on *Forever Amber*. The studio rejected the suggestion. Two more attempts were made a few years later. In December 1979, CBS wanted to develop a four-hour television project based on *Forever Amber* in conjunction with Fox TV. Three months after that, in March 1980, the BBC approached Fox TV hoping to co-produce a mini-series based on the material. Nothing ever happened with either of these projects.

The last heard-of attempt to remake *Forever Amber* was in 1986 when Raquel Welch announced that she planned to produce and star in a TV mini-series based on the novel. On May 7, 1986, *The Hollywood Reporter's* "Rambling Reporter" ran a brief piece in which Kathleen Winsor was asked what she thought of 44-year-old Raquel playing 16-year-old Amber. Ms. Winsor replied: "I'm not going to start finding fault with Raquel Welch. I don't believe I've ever seen her. She's probably as suitable for the part as anybody. Think of all the actresses who've played Juliet, and she's 14." The project was mentioned several times in the press over the

Linda Darnell and Cornel Wilde.

next few months and then never again. When asked to comment on it for this book, Ms. Welch declined to respond.

As of this writing, no uncut print of the film has been found, although the unedited original dialogue track still exists. When Fox released *Forever Amber* on video in 1994, the original soundtrack was restored but, since the final scene between Amber and Nan was cut from the negative, the sound at the end of the film simply fades out, which makes for a very unsatisfying conclusion. In this respect, it would have been better to hear Bruce's final voiceover from the altered version. At least it gives the movie some sense of finality. Hopefully somewhere an unedited print of *Forever Amber* still exists and will surface so that the film can once again be seen as it should be. To date the film has only been released on a studio-authorized DVD in Spain from Impulso Records and Films.

The character of Amber St. Clare returned to popular literature in *The League of Extraordinary Gentlemen*, which began in 1999 as a comic book series. Written by Alan Moore and illustrated by Kevin O'Neill, Moore has described the work as a "Justice League of Victorian England," referring to the Justice League of America whose members include such DC superheroes as Superman, Batman, and Wonder Woman. As the Moore/O'Neill series progressed, a myriad of fictional literary characters began to appear in the stories. A backstory relates that the roots of the League began in the 17th Century as "Prospero's Men," founded in 1610 by the character of that name from Shakespeare's *The Tempest*. Some of the other members of this group are Ariel and Caliban (also characters from *The Tempest*), Cervantes' Don Quixote, Virginia Woolf's Orlando, and Kathleen Winsor's Amber St. Clare. In the 2007 graphic novel

The League of Extraordinary Gentlemen: Black Dossier, Amber appears as a brothel madam in a fabricated sequel to John Cleland's 1748 novel *Fanny Hill*.

Sheet Music for Forever Amber.

CHAPTER TWELVE
The Musical Score

WHEN THE FIRST VERSION OF *FOREVER AMBER* WAS IN production, Alfred Newman, the head of the Fox Music Department, was set to score the picture. When the production was delayed, Newman proceeded with his plans to score *Captain from Castile*, which would require a great deal of music. By the time filming on the final version of *Forever Amber* was completed, *Captain from Castile* was already in post-production and set to open a month after *Forever Amber*. Newman realized that he couldn't possibly write the music for both films so he set about searching for another composer he felt could do justice to a motion picture as large scale as *Forever Amber*. He decided to approach Erich Wolfgang Korngold, who had retired from film scoring at Warner Bros. the previous year to pursue more "serious composition." Normally, Newman would not have gone outside his "stable" of Fox studio composers, but he knew *Forever Amber* was an important picture and much of the studio's fortune was depending on its success. Korngold had a great deal of experience scoring large-scale costume pictures, including *The Adventures of Robin Hood*, *Captain Blood*, and *The Private Lives of Elizabeth and Essex*. Unfortunately, Korngold had to decline because of ill health and Newman was forced to look elsewhere. At the suggestion of Otto Preminger, Newman decided on David Raksin.

David Raksin (1912-2004) had come to Hollywood in 1935 to assist Charlie Chaplin in the scoring of *Modern Times*. When the two disagreed, Chaplin fired him, but Alfred Newman, who was conducting the score, intervened and convinced Chaplin to let Raksin stay on. When Newman became head of the music department at 20th Century-Fox in 1940, Raksin became a composer for the studio at Newman's behest. At first Raksin was a second-tier composer, writing the background music for Fox programmers such as *The Undying Monster* and *Dr. Renault's Secret* (both 1942). When Raksin was hired to write the music for *Laura* (1944), Otto Preminger wanted to use Duke Ellington's song "Sophisticated Lady" as the theme for the title character. Instead, Raksin composed an original theme which became one of the most recognizable pieces of music in the history of the movies, and contributed greatly to the eventual success of the film. A song version with lyrics by Johnny Mercer enjoyed even more widespread popularity. Preminger requested Raksin to score his film *Fallen Angel* the following year.

Forever Amber would be the "biggest" production that David Raksin had yet worked on and, unlike his most of his other films, it was not set in contemporary times. While the score for *Laura* had been largely mono-thematic, the music for *Forever Amber* would require far more variety. Also, the running time of the film dictated that the score would be a lengthy one. Despite his commitment to *Captain from Castile*, Alfred Newman continued to closely supervise Raksin's progress. The result of Newman's continued involvement is evident in the quality of the end product which reflects his influence.

David Raksin took his initial inspiration from the music of Henry Purcell and the late Baroque era. Raksin later said of the score, "I knew that to the perspective audience the music that says 'England' is not that which was being composed there during the reign of Charles II but rather music written half a century later by a German, George Frederic Handel... therefore I decided that I would try to evoke the required atmosphere by playing upon certain musical mannerisms generally thought of as 'English.'" In a 1998 radio interview with Raksin, actress Jane Greer made the observation: "About two thirds of David's [*Forever Amber*] score is derived from one musical idea; a repeating bass line around which he builds his various melodies and harmonies." British radio broadcaster and film music critic Robert Reynolds says: "Bass line is the lowest note of a chord. In a symphonic structure this bass line is built around the double basses which gives the lowest pitch. In other words Mr. Raksin did indeed build his entire score around the sound from the lowest keyed instrument in his orchestra — the double bass."

Raksin was originally supposed to have twelve weeks in which to compose the score but three and a half weeks after he was given the assignment, the picture was still being cut. Now with only eight and a half weeks in order to meet the deadline set for the film's planned October release, Raksin was forced to move into high gear. He finished the score in just under two months, working everyday, often from 7 am to 1 am. According to studio publicity, Raksin averaged two minutes of music per day, which was then considered a record in film composition. When it was completed, the score ran 450 pages with an approximate running time of 118 minutes. The score was then orchestrated by Maurice de Packh, Herbert Spencer, and an uncredited Edward Powell. On August 21, 1947, Fox released a studio memo saying that a 100-piece symphony orchestra conducted by Alfred Newman had just finished recording the background music of *Forever Amber*.

David Raksin got his chance to conduct the music he had composed for *Forever Amber* shortly thereafter as, on September 14, he led a 78-piece orchestra at Republic Studios in a recording of the score. The recording was for a soundtrack album to be distributed by RCA Victor in conjunction with the film's release. On September 19, Raksin contacted the Fox legal department and requested that he be paid 9 cents royalty per album. Fox was to receive 18 cents per album from RCA Victor and the studio had previously agreed to pay Raksin 40% (7.2 cents) of that. Since Fox had footed the $9,000 bill for the recording, they reasoned that they should have the greater percentage of the profits and his request was denied.

At this point in time, soundtrack albums were not commonplace, but RCA had enjoyed considerable success with their album of Dimitri Tiomkin's score for *Duel in the Sun* the previous year so a trend was being established. The album of *Forever Amber* contained three 78rpm discs with six themes from the score: Amber, The King's Mistress, Whitefriars Music, The Idyll at Chiverton Cottage, The Great Fire of London, and Forever Amber.

Sheet music for the main theme with lyrics by Johnny Mercer was also released in an attempt to duplicate the success of the song from *Laura*. The sheet music eventually created a problem when another composer claimed that he had written the theme. On December 20, 1947, the Fox legal department responded to his charge with a correspondence which stated: "The composition, *Forever Amber*, by David Raksin, lyric by Johnny Mercer, is based on a theme from the picture known as 'The Wench.' The above composition is actually 'The Wench' theme played through twice, arranged of course, in Fox Trot form."

> *"Forever Amber, she gave a moment a name to remember.*
> *One glance from Amber your heart within you became as warm as*
> *candle flame."*
>
> Lyric by Johnny Mercer

The song did not duplicate the success of "Laura" and is mostly forgotten today. The score, however, garnered the film its only Academy Award nomination. The nomination was well deserved, but *Forever Amber* lost the award to Miklos Rozsa's score for *A Double Life*. Alfred Newman's music for *Captain from Castile* was also among the nominees that year.

The music from *Forever Amber* did become a favorite of film music enthusiasts and long after its original release, the 78rpm album became a much-sought-after collector's item. For many years the only way to hear the score was on a bootleg LP in which it was paired with the *Duel in the Sun* album. In 1975, David Raksin was asked to conduct a suite of themes from *Forever Amber* for the outstanding RCA Victor "Classic Film Scores" series, produced by Charles Gerhardt. Raksin was excited at the prospect and put together a suite which included all the themes from the original 78rpm discs with the exception of "The Idyll at Chiverton Cottage." It was recorded in London with Raksin conducting the New Philharmonic Orchestra in October 1975.

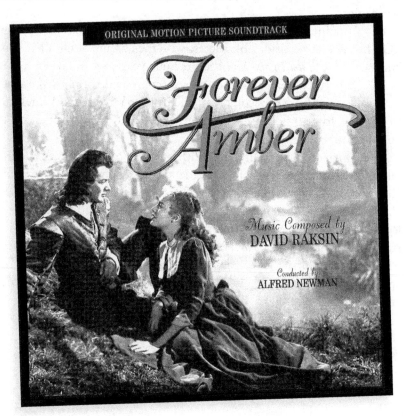

The Varese Sarabande soundtrack CD.

In later years Rakin never seemed to miss an opportunity to deride the film of *Forever Amber*, although he did admit that the score was one of his favorites. Although he went on to score many other notable movies, he never again scored a film of its magnitude. In his liner notes for the "Classic Film Scores" recording he says, in part, "Twenty-eight years after its first appearance, what was then a disappointment to its parents and its public had become a paragon of 'kitsch & sync.' Not that 'Amber' was a first-rate example of the genre, but it was rich and self indulgent in a way that calls for the composer to go all out."

It took Varese Sarabande and its "Fox Classics" collection on CD to release the definitive recording of the *Forever Amber* score in 1998. This recording is taken from the original music tracks and consists of four lengthy suites which, according to the notes, were compiled from over 100 individual cues. The resulting CD is, in a word, magnificent. Special credit must be given to the late Rick Victor for his superb job of mixing, editing, and assembling the score for this recording.

In his otherwise excellent liner notes for the Varese Sarabande CD, Jon Burlingame unfortunately cannot resist making a jibe at the film: "[The music] would, in fact, be better remembered than the film for which it was written." Actually, other than among film score buffs, this is debatable. Burlingame goes on to say: "The *Forever Amber* score contains a wealth of diverse material and intricate writing, making it among the richest and most expressive music for any American film of its time. David Raksin's *Forever Amber* remains one of Hollywood's musical masterpieces."

CHAPTER THIRTEEN
Restoration Theatre

THE THEATRE PLAYS A VERY IMPORTANT PART IN THE STORY of Amber St. Clare, and in the history of England as well. In 1642, the Civil War between the Puritan Parliamentarians and the Royalists broke out in England and, on September 2 that same year, Parliament issued a declaration suppressing the performance of stage plays. In 1648, the Parliamentarians ordered the destruction of all theaters and the arrest and punishment of all actors. Anyone caught attending a play was fined. The following year, King Charles I was beheaded and England was now under Puritan rule. During the entire reign of the Puritan leader Oliver Cromwell, all theatre in England was suppressed as sinful. Cromwell died in 1658 and two years later Charles II was restored to the throne.

The Restoration period allowed the English people to throw off the confining shackles of the Puritan rule and embrace the luxuries and frivolities they had been denied for so long. King Charles II was a great fan of theatricals and in 1662 he licensed two theatre companies. "His Majesty's Players" performed in the King's Theatre at Drury Lane under the management of Thomas Killigrew. "His Highness's Comedians" were under the management a Mr. Davenant in the Duke of York's Theatre at Lincoln's Inn. There were other companies as well, but these were not sanctioned by the throne and therefore the performances were not

Harry, Amber, and Bruce attend a theatrical performance.

considered legal. The two most famous players of the time were Charles Hart, who had continued to act throughout the Puritan regime, and Edward Kynaston, the actor whom writer Samuel Pepys once called "the most beautiful woman on the London stage." Kynaston was one of "His Majesty's Players" and, since women were prohibited from performing on the stage, he had gained great fame for enacting women's roles. Shortly after reopening the theaters, King Charles also lifted the ban on stage performances by women. A number of actresses took to "the boards," including fictional Amber St. Clare, who is presented to Thomas Killigrew by Edward Kynaston in the novel.

The theatre became closely associated with the Court of King Charles II for a number of reasons. First, Charles was a rabid theatergoer. It is estimated that he attended over four hundred plays during his twenty-five years on the throne. Second, although Shakespeare's plays were extremely popular so were the new "Restoration Comedies," often written by members of the Court such as Sir Charles Sedley, Sir George Etherege, and even George Villiers, the Duke of Buckingham. These ribald comedies were a reflection of the attitudes of the times and greatly appealed to the people. Lastly, King Charles had a great fondness for actresses. In 1668 Charles made the acquaintance of the actresses Nell Gwynne and Moll Davis at the Tunbridge Wells spa. Moll Davis became his mistress for a time, but he soon tired of her. Nell Gwynne, on the other hand, began a relationship with him that endured until his death in 1685. Nell had started as an "orange girl" at the King's Theatre in Drury Lane and later graduated to an actress of some repute. Samuel Pepys wrote of her: "So great a performance of a comical part was never in the world before as Nell do this." She bore Charles a son who became the first Duke of St. Albans. On his deathbed, Charles instructed his brother James to "let not poor Nelly starve," but she was soon relegated to obscurity and died two years after Charles.

In 2004, an entertaining, if not historically accurate, movie called *Stage Beauty* was released. Based on Jeffrey Hatcher's play *Compleat Female Stage Beauty*, the plot revolves around the character of Edward "Ned" Kynaston (well played by Billy Crudup). Kynaston runs afoul of King Charles' mistress Nell Gwynne, who is an aspiring actress. She convinces the King to lift the ban on women performing in the theatre and make it illegal for men to impersonate women on stage. This effectively puts Kynaston out of work but helps to make a star out of his former dresser, Maria (Claire Danes). Maria, who has been studying her employer's acting techniques, quickly moves into his roles.

Stage Beauty presents a fascinating portrait of the times and includes a number of historical persons such as Samuel Pepys (Hugh Bonneville) and George Villiers (Ben Chaplin). Villiers is shown as having been Kynaston's lover, which apparently is accurate. Other characterizations do not ring so true. Rupert Everett's King Charles II is a silly fop, which the real Charles definitely was not. There is no mention of Sir Charles Sedley

Amber onstage.

(Richard Griffiths) as a playwright and instead he is presented merely as a grotesque and vindictive courtier. Although Zoe Tapper's spirited performance as Nell Gwynne is a good one, the real Nell had already been an actress before she became Charles' mistress. These quibbles aside, the film is well directed by Richard Eyre from a screenplay adapted by Jeffrey Hatcher from his play. However, the movie's greatest success lies in the performance of Billy Crudup as Edward Kynaston. Crudup manages to effectively maintain Kynaston's sexual ambiguity despite the script's lame attempts to suggest that he may have been "converted" to heterosexuality in the end.

Most of the real personages connected with the theatre who are mentioned above appear in the novel of *Forever Amber*. Some of them are also are in various versions of the screenplays, including the characters of Edward Kynaston, Sir Charles Sedley, and Thomas Killigrew. Sedley is, in fact, one of the characters on the casting lists for the first version. Only Killigrew (played by Tom Moore) made it into the final film. In the scripts, the theatre where Amber is employed is incorrectly referred to as either "His Majesty's Theatre" or "Theatre Royal" instead of the King's Theatre. Whatever the name, the theatre sequences in *Forever Amber* are some of the most memorable in the film and successfully convey the rowdy, chaotic atmosphere that typified the Restoration theatre experience.

CHAPTER FOURTEEN

Biographical Notes

MARI ALDON
(1929-2004)

In 1946 Mari Aldon came to Hollywood from Toronto, Canada, where she had already been a ballet dancer and then a radio actress for the Canadian Broadcasting Corporation. Fox studio publicity claimed that she had come to Hollywood specifically to obtain a role in *Forever Amber*; however, she did play an uncredited bit part in the R.K.O. film *The Locket* (1946) prior to her being cast as Bess Columbine. Neither she nor her character made it into the final version of *Forever Amber*. Over the next several years she continued to play uncredited parts in films. In 1951 she was suddenly elevated to leading lady status opposite Gary

Mari Aldon as Bess Columbine.

Cooper in Warner Bros.' *Distant Drums*. She remained at Warners for a supporting part in the Joan Crawford starrer *This Woman is Dangerous* (1952). In 1954 she appeared in a supporting role in *The Barefoot Contessa* and went to England to star with Richard Conte in the pre-horror Hammer Film *Mask of Dust* (released in the U.S. as *A Race for Life*). Following an appearance in David Lean's *Summertime* (1955), she turned her attention to television, where she continued to appear in programs until 1966.

PATI BEHRS
(1922-2004)

Actress Pati Behrs is an interesting footnote in the filming of *Forever Amber*. Born in Russia, she was the daughter of Prince Andre Behrs, a colonel in the Czar's Royal Cavalry, and the grandniece of Leo Tolstoy. During World War II she acquired a considerable reputation as a cabaret entertainer in Paris. As such, she was brought to Hollywood by Fox with the intention of casting her as the Countess of Castlemaine in *Forever Amber*. The part eventually went to Natalie Draper and instead Pati played an uncredited bit in *The Razor's Edge* (1946). Pati did appear in the second version of *Forever Amber* in the miniscule role of Amber's French makeup artist. At least she had a line, even if it was in French. She continued as a Fox contract player, appearing in *Apartment for Peggy, When My Baby Smiles at Me,* and *Unfaithfully Yours* (all 1948). Her final film was *Come to the Stable* in 1949. She became John Derek's first wife in 1951 and retired from show business to raise their two children.

JEROME "JERRY" CADY
(1903-1948)

Jerome Cady began his Hollywood career as a staff writer for Fox. During his first tenure there, from 1937 to 1939, he wrote a number of programmers. Cady moved over to R.K.O., but once again he was saddled with the studio's "B" product. Returning to Fox in 1942, he found his niche writing war films such as *Guadalcanal Diary* (1943), *The Purple Heart* (1944), and *A Wing and a Prayer* (1944). He received an Academy Award nomination for the latter, which led to his writing assignment on *Forever Amber*. He wrote a lengthy treatment (for which he received an "adaptation" screen credit) and the first versions of the script. After being taken off *Forever Amber*, he wrote the "boy and his dog" movie, *Thunder in the Valley* (1947). He next penned what is probably his most famous film, *Call Northside 777* (1948). For this screenplay he was nominated for a Screen Writers Guild of America Award and won the Edgar Allan Poe Award for Best Screenplay. Sadly, he was not around to enjoy this acclaim. On November 7, 1948, Jerome Cady sailed his yacht to Catalina Island where he anchored and then committed suicide.

PEGGY CUMMINS
(1925-)

In a brief article entitled "Amber Notes" in the July 1947 issue of *Photoplay* it states that Fox wasn't dropping "the innocent-faced, little blond beauty…She's going into *Bob, Son of Battle*. Bosses know they've found real talent in the young lady and intend using her where she'll show

Peggy Cummins as Amber St. Clare.

to best advantage." *Bob, Son of Battle* eventually became *Thunder in the Valley* (1947) with Peggy Ann Garner in the female lead. Instead, Peggy Cummins was "Introduced" in *The Late George Apley* (1947) playing the important supporting role of Ronald Colman's daughter Ellie. Her performance was good enough to elevate her to the star of her next film, *Moss Rose* (1947). In this Victorian melodrama she plays a Cockney chorus girl who becomes involved with murder, blackmail, and Victor Mature. Also featured were two of her *Forever Amber* alumnae, Vincent Price and Margo Woode. Peggy received many favorable reviews for this performance. A typical example appeared in *The San Francisco California News*: "Miss Cummins is excellent…It's a pleasure to find a pretty newcomer to films who can act as well as decorate the celluloid." In 1948 she made two other films under her Fox contract, *Escape* with Rex Harrison and *Green Grass of Wyoming*. In 1949 she played what is probably the finest part of her career, in the United Artists release *Gun Crazy*. In this excellent *film noir*, Peggy and John Dall are "Bonnie and Clyde"-type gangsters on the run. Afterwards, she returned to England where she continued her acting career, most notably in the classic horror film *Curse of the Demon* (1958).

LINDA DARNELL
(1923-1965)

As soon as her work on *Forever Amber* was completed, Linda Darnell went to Europe for a brief vacation. When she returned, she began filming *The Walls of Jericho*. In January 1948, while that film was in production, Linda and her husband Pev Marley adopted a baby girl whom they named Lola. Linda next played a memorable role in Preston Sturges' dark comedy *Unfaithfully Yours* (1948). She followed this with *A Letter to Three Wives* (1949), in which she gave what many feel was the finest performance of her career. The movie was both a critical and popular success but, although Linda now had the child she had wanted so badly and recognition for her acting abilities, her marriage to Pev Marley was in trouble. Linda had fallen in love with director Joseph Mankiewicz while filming *A Letter to Three Wives* and her often stormy marriage to Marley finally came to an end in 1951. Linda hoped that she and Mankiewicz would marry, but he was already married and would not leave his wife for her. She never got over him and considered him to be the "love of her life." When 20th Century-Fox cancelled Linda's contract in September 1952, she went on to freelance at other studios. She married twice more, to Philip Liebmann, head of the Rheingold Beer Company, and to Merle "Robby" Robertson, an American Airlines pilot. Both marriages ended in divorce. After *Zero*

Hour! in 1957, movie offers for Linda were nonexistent so she concentrated on theatre and nightclub work. In 1964 she returned to films in a supporting role in the Paramount Western *Black Spurs*. Following a tour of the play *Janus* in early 1965, Linda decided to spend the Easter holidays with some friends in Chicago. While she was visiting, a fire broke out in their home and Linda was trapped inside. She was badly burned and died on April 10, 1965. Her final film, *Black Spurs*, opened in theaters six weeks after her death. Although some contemporary sources claim that Linda Darnell's career suffered because of *Forever Amber*, the roles she played in the years following it were some of the best of her entire career and she brought to them an assurance she had not exhibited in the past.

Linda Darnell as Amber St. Clare.

WILLIAM "WEE WILLIE" DAVIS
(1906-1981)

New York-born William Davis' main claim to fame was as a professional wrestler during the Thirties and Forties, but he was a prolific character actor in films as well. He made his uncredited movie debut in *Shadow of the Thin Man* (1941) and graduated to a larger role, with billing, in Cecil B. DeMille's *Reap the Wild Wind* the following year. He became something of a staple in the Maria Montez/Jon Hall films at Universal, appearing in *Arabian Nights* (1942), *Ali Baba and the Forty Thieves* (1944), and *Gypsy Wildcat* (1944). Following his unseen stint as "Big John Waterman" in *Forever Amber*, he went into the Fox film *The*

Wee Willie Davis as Big John Waterman.

Foxes of Harrow (1947), directed by John M. Stahl. He appeared as himself opposite *Mighty Joe Young* (1949) and went on to play small parts in such high-profile films as *Samson and Delilah* (1949) and *The Asphalt Jungle* (1950). His last film was Alfred Hitchcock's *To Catch a Thief* (1955), after which he became a wrestling promoter in Louisville, Kentucky. He has sometimes been confused with the William "Wee Willie" Davis who was a songwriter and played piano for Louis Jordan and His Band, the Tympany Five.

RALPH FAULKNER
(1891-1987)

Ralph Faulkner began his career in movies as an actor in 1917. Following a knee injury in 1922, he took up fencing as a form of therapeutic exercise. He became fascinated with the sport and eventually became a member of the U.S. Olympic fencing team in both 1928 and 1932. Combining his acting career with his love of fencing, he appeared in such classic swashbucklers as *The Three Musketeers* and *Captain Blood* (both 1935). The first film in which he choreographed the fight sequences was *The Prisoner of Zenda* (1937). In 1945 he was the fencing master on Columbia's *The Bandit of Sherwood Forest*, which starred Cornel Wilde on loan out from Fox. Wilde had been a national intercollegiate fencing champion and he and Faulkner got along famously during the shooting of the picture. When Faulkner signed on for *Forever Amber* in December 1945, it was planned that he would play a small part, but his main function was to instruct the other actors in the art of swordplay. By the time *Forever Amber* went into production for the second time, Faulkner was busy elsewhere as the fight coordinator for *The Fighting Guardsman* and *Wife of Monte Cristo* (both 1946). Fred Cavens, who was hired as a technical advisor, became the fencing master for the completed version of *Forever Amber*. Throughout the next several decades Ralph Faulkner continued to appear in and choreograph the fight scenes for movies and to teach fencing at his Falcon Studios in Hollywood. Among his numerous credits are *The Virgin Queen* (1955), *The Court Jester* (1956), and *Jason and the Argonauts* (1963). In the latter, he worked with stop-motion animation genius Ray Harryhausen to choreograph many of the complicated special effects sequences involving swordplay. Faulkner's final film work was performing a similar task on Harryhausen's last film, *Clash of the Titans* (1981). He continued to teach fencing at his studio until his death in 1987.

MARGOT GRAHAME
(1911–1982)

Margot Grahame made her movie debut in 1930 and was soon touted as the "British Jean Harlow." She married actor Francis Lister in 1934 and came with him to Hollywood when MGM offered him a role in *Mutiny on the Bounty* (1935). Meanwhile, Margot went to R.K.O. where she tested for and won the part of Victor McLaglen's girlfriend in *The Informer* (1935). R.K.O. signed her to a contract and that same year she appeared in the 1935 version of *The Three Musketeers* as the evil Lady De Winter. When her husband decided to return to England, she declined to go with him and they divorced in early 1936. R.K.O. cast her in a series

Margot Grahame as Bess Columbine.

of mediocre roles and in 1937 she bought herself out of her contract. Her next part was in Cecil B. DeMille's *The Buccaneer* (1938). Shortly thereafter, she married a second time and spent the next several years living in Canada and England, concentrating on stage work. She divorced again in 1946 and returned to Hollywood. Margot Grahame's involvement with *Forever Amber* has been speculated about and generally misconstrued. Sources usually claim that she was going to be in the first attempt (either as the Countess of Castlemaine or Bess Columbine) but wasn't retained for the second version. Actually, she signed her contract to appear in *Forever Amber* as "Bess" on September 26, 1946, months after the first production had been shut down. Her first day of shooting was November 30, 1946. She completed all of her scenes in six days for which she was paid the unusual amount of $1,666.67. She returned on December 16 to do an interior coach process shot to be used during the coach holdup sequence. In the proposed "Screen and Advertising Credits" for *Forever Amber* submitted on March 17 and April 16, 1947, her name is featured prominently in the cast. In a similar cast and credits listing of May 17, 1947, her name is no longer mentioned and there is no sign of her in the final release version of the film. Immediately after her involvement with *Forever Amber*, Margot appeared in *The Fabulous Joe* (1947) for United Artists, after which she returned to England. Her final film was *St. Joan* (1957) working with her *Forever Amber* director Otto Preminger. On New Year's Day, 1982, she died in her London home where she had been a recluse for several years.

RICHARD GREENE
(1918-1985)

Richard Greene was born into an acting family and made his stage debut at age 19 with a bit part in the play *Journey's End*. Two years later he had graduated to the juvenile lead in the London stage production of Terence Rattigan's *French Without Tears*. While appearing in this play, Richard was spotted by a 20th Century-Fox talent scout. In January 1938, he was signed to a Fox contract and brought to Hollywood to appear in the John Ford film *Four Men and a Prayer* (1938). He received excellent notices, which prompted Fox to cast him in three more pictures that year. The following year he appeared in four more Fox films, most notably *The Hound of the Baskervilles* starring Basil Rathbone as Sherlock Holmes. Although his star power was growing, in 1940 Greene asked to be released from his Fox contract so he could return to England and fight in the War. He enlisted that year and remained on active duty until December 1944. During his time in the service, he married actress Patricia Medina and brought her back to Hollywood with him when he returned in 1946. He was one of the top three choices to play Bruce Carlton when casting suggestions were being made for the first version of *Forever Amber*. His wife was also under consideration for the part of Bruce's wife Corinna. Neither of them made it into that film but when the movie resumed production, Richard replaced Vincent Price as Harry Almsbury. He was pleased to be playing what was essentially a character part and hoped it would lead to more diverse roles than he had been offered during his previous stint in Hollywood. Instead, he became typecast in costume pictures. He continued to freelance at various studios but when film offers became scarce he turned to television. He gained his greatest success in the series *The*

Richard Greene as Harry Almsbury.

Adventures of Robin Hood, which began in 1955 and ran four years. He later brought this character to the big screen when he co-produced and starred in *Sword of Sherwood Forest* (1961) for Britain's Hammer Films. His last film was *Tales from the Crypt* in 1972, but he continued to work in television for the next ten years. In 1982 Richard underwent surgery for a brain tumor, but he never completely recovered from this and died in 1985.

RICHARD HAYDN
(1905-1985)

George Richard Haydon was born in London where he was a stage revue star during the Thirties. In 1938 he traveled to the United States to

Richard Haydn as the Earl of Radclyffe.

appear with Beatrice Lillie in the Broadway production of Noel Coward's *Set to Music*. His motion picture debut was in the R.K.O. film *Ball of Fire* (1941). He usually played lightweight comedy character roles using his trademark adenoidal method of delivering lines. This was best exemplified when he voiced the "Caterpillar" for Disney's animated feature *Alice in Wonderland* (1951). When he was cast against type as the iniquitous "Earl of Radclyffe" in the first version of *Forever Amber*, he wanted to play the role so badly that, when the film stopped production, he went to great lengths to assure he would again be considered for the part when filming resumed. In 1948 Richard Haydn directed and appeared in *Miss Tatlock's Millions*, a screwball comedy for Paramount. He remained at Paramount, where he also directed *Dear Wife* (1949) and *Mr. Music* (1950). Although his stint as a director was brief, he maintained a lengthy career in both movies and television as a reliable supporting player. In later years he appeared in such diverse films as *The Lost World* (1960), *Mutiny on the Bounty* (1962), and *The Sound of Music* (1965). His final film role was in Mel Brooks' *Young Frankenstein* (1974).

GLENN LANGAN
(1917-1991)

An August 18, 1945, syndicated newspaper article by Rosalind Shaffer summed up much of what can be said about Glenn Langan: "Being young, good looking, well trained and talented isn't enough, without luck, to make the grade in show business. For proof just take the case of Glenn Langan." Thomas Glenn Langan was born in Denver, Colorado, in 1917. The handsome 6'4" actor made his uncredited movie debut in the 1939 Warner Bros. short subject *The Bill of Rights*. He continued at Warners for another five films in 1939 and finally achieved an onscreen credit for his small role in *The Return of Doctor X* starring Humphrey Bogart. Glenn left Hollywood and went to New York where he got a part in the 1942 Broadway revival of James M. Barrie's *A Kiss for Cinderella* which featured Luise Rainer. Upon returning to Hollywood he was signed to a studio contract at 20th Century-Fox and made his debut there in *Four Jills in a Jeep* (1944). He eventually appeared in more than a dozen films at Fox, including his memorable stint as Rex Morgan in both versions of *Forever Amber*. A sad comment on his tenure at Fox was that after appearing in a number of pictures for the studio his name was mentioned to Darryl Zanuck who responded, "Who's Glenn Langan?" Glenn's contract with Fox ended with *The Snake Pit* in 1949. The following year he starred in *The Treasure of Monte Cristo* opposite Adele Jergens. The couple fell in love and married in 1951. Glenn continued to appear in movies and television for the next two decades. His greatest claim to fame was as the tragic Col. Glenn Manning in *The Amazing Colossal Man* (1957), a science-fiction B movie by producer/director Bert I. Gordon. Langan gives an impressive performance as a man whose exposure to the blast of a plutonium bomb causes him to grow into a giant. Few such movies of the period could boast acting of this caliber. Another memorable gig for Glenn came in 1967 when he appeared as a semi-regular on the ABC television series *Hondo*. His final movie was *The Andromeda Strain* in 1971. He died of cancer in 1991 in Camarillo, California, with his wife of forty years, Adele, by his side.

Glenn Langan as Rex Morgan.

RING LARDNER, JR
(1915-2000)

In the spring of 1947, Ring Lardner Jr. was forced to interrupt his work on the script of *Forever Amber* as he had been summoned to appear before the House UnAmerican Activities Committee in Washington D.C. After graduating from Princeton University, Lardner had gone to the Soviet Union to study. He returned and became a reporter, first for the *New York Herald-Tribune* and later for the *New York Daily Mirror*. While living in New York, he joined the Communist Party. In 1935, Lardner moved to Hollywood and became a publicity writer and story editor for David O. Selznick. After working on the script for *Nothing Sacred* (1937), he moved to Warner Bros., but his time there was short lived because of his political activities. Lardner had continued to attend Communist Party meetings in Hollywood. Because of his politics, work at the studios was sporadic. It was only at the intervention of Katharine Hepburn that he was given a writing credit on *Woman of the Year* (1942), for which he won an Academy Award. When Lardner appeared before the H.U.A.C. in 1947, he refused to discuss whether or not he had any Communist Party affiliations and he also would not provide names of any other members. He attempted to read into the record a statement declaring that the Committee was attacking the freedom of American citizens, but was repeatedly prevented from doing so. The Committee labeled him a "hostile witness." When Lardner returned to Fox to continue work on *Forever Amber*, Darryl F. Zanuck immediately fired him. Lardner was blacklisted and become one of the "Hollywood Ten" screenwriters who were sent to prison for contempt. After his release from prison, Lardner moved to Mexico. In 1954 he returned to the U.S. and began to do uncredited writing for television beginning with *The Adventures of Robin Hood* series which starred Richard Greene. He wrote scripts for films either using pseudonyms or without credit as in the case of Otto Preminger's *The Cardinal* (1963). He finally received a writing credit in his own name for *The Cincinnati Kid* in 1965. In 1970 he won his second Academy Award for Robert Altman's *M*A*S*H*. His final script was for *The Greatest* (1977).

VINCENT PRICE
(1911-1993)

Several years prior to being cast in *Forever Amber*, Vincent Price had appeared as "King Charles II" in the Fox film *Hudson's Bay* (1941). This has caused a number of film references to assume he was going to play the same part in *Forever Amber*, which he was not. When Darryl F. Zanuck shut down production on the first version of *Forever Amber*, Price was loaned out to R.K.O. for *The Long Night* (1947). Afterwards, he returned to Fox to appear with his *Forever Amber* co-star Peggy Cummins in *Moss Rose* (1947). Ms. Cummins and Price had an excellent working relationship and, in later years, always spoke of each other in the most glowing terms. Zanuck next cast him in *Captain from Castile* in the role of the villainous "Diego de Silva," but Price found the part extremely unappealing and refused to play it (John Sutton did). Zanuck responded by letting the option on Price's Fox contract lapse. The following year he was back in 17th-century garb as "Richelieu" in the lavish MGM version of *The Three Musketeers* (1948). Fear of reprisals from the Catholic Church

Vincent Price as Harry Almsbury.

(again!) prevented MGM from referring to Richelieu as "Cardinal" in the script and from showing him in clerical robes, but Price's slyly sinister characterization was one of the very best things in the movie. This was only a hint of villainous parts to come for an actor who would enjoy one of the longest and brightest careers in motion pictures.

JOHN RUSSELL
(1921–1991)

Los Angeles-born John Russell was an outstanding athlete while he was student at U.C.L.A. After college he enlisted in the Marine Corp during WWII and was decorated for valorous conduct at Guadalcanal.

John Russell as Black Jack Mallard.

He was later wounded and given a medical discharge from active duty. Back in Los Angeles a talent scout spotted John in a restaurant and his good looks earned him a 20th Century-Fox contract. His first film was *A Royal Scandal* (1945). He appeared in six more Fox pictures before being cast in the important role of "Black Jack" in the second version of *Forever Amber.* His last film for Fox was *Slattery's Hurricane* (1949), which also starred Linda Darnell. John went on to appear frequently in movies and television, more often than not in Westerns. His greatest fame came when he starred as Marshal Dan Troop in the TV series *Lawman,* which ran from 1958 to 1962. His last film was *Under the Gun* in 1988. John Russell always remained proud of his participation in *Forever Amber.* Discussing the film in 1987 he had praise for his "outstanding colleagues" and the "overall technical excellence" of the production.

GEORGE SANDERS
(1906-1972)

George Henry Sanders was born to English parents in St. Petersburg, Russia. The family fled back to Britain during the Russian Revolution. George attended Brighton College and Manchester Technical College with the intention of going into the textile industry. Instead, he decided to pursue a career as an actor. In 1934 he landed a part in the Noel Coward play *Conversation Piece* and made his motion picture debut as an uncredited singer in *Love, Life, and Laughter.* Two years later he graduated to a leading role in the British film *Strange Cargo.*

At this point George decided to leave England and try his luck in Hollywood. His first part in Hollywood was a showy supporting performance in *Lloyds of London* (1937), which landed him a 20th Century-Fox contract. This was the first of five movies he would eventually make with Tyrone Power, including Power's unfinished final film *Solomon and Sheba* (1959). In 1939 George was loaned by Fox to R.K.O. to play the part of detective Simon Templar in *The Saint Strikes Back.* He would enact this role in five films. When George tired of playing The Saint, the part was given to actor Hugh Sinclair. R.K.O. then cast George as Gay Lawrence, a.k.a. "The Falcon," in another series of detective movies which began with *The Gay Falcon* (1941). He played The Falcon in four films before turning the part over to his older brother Tom Conway (1904-1967) in *The Falcon's Brother* (1942). Among George Sanders' many notable films are *Rebecca* and *Foreign Correspondent* (both directed by Alfred Hitchcock in 1940), *The Moon and Sixpence* (1942), and *Summer Storm* (1944), in which he starred opposite Linda Darnell in what became her breakout dramatic role. When *Forever Amber* resumed filming, George replaced Reginald Gardiner in the part of King Charles II. He would play this character again, though far less effectively, in MGM's CinemaScope swashbuckler *The King's Thief* (1955). He won a well deserved Best Supporting Actor Academy Award for his portrayal of the poison-tongued Addison DeWitt in *All About Eve* (1950). George Sanders committed suicide in Barcelona, Spain, in 1972 leaving a now famous suicide note which read in part, "Dear World, I am leaving because I am bored." His final screen role was in the British horror movie *Psychomania*, which was released the year after his death.

George Sanders as King Charles II.

JOHN M. STAHL
(1886-1950)

Although he had an extremely lengthy and diverse career in motion pictures, John M. Stahl is unjustly not remembered today as having been a major force in the industry. John Stahl began working in films in 1914 and, throughout the ensuing years, alternately performed duties as producer, writer and director. He was also one of the founding members of the Academy of Motion Picture Arts and Sciences. During the Thirties he most notably directed the original versions of *Imitation of Life* (1934) and *Magnificent Obsession* (1935). He was a freelance director until 1943 when he signed on with 20th Century-Fox to helm *Immortal Sergeant.* He remained with the studio until his death. During his years with Fox, Stahl was responsible for a number of noteworthy films, but his most famous achievement remains *Leave Her to Heaven* (1945). He had been responsible for bringing the novel to the attention of Darryl F. Zanuck. Following his unsuccessful participation in *Forever Amber*, he was immediately assigned another costume drama based on a popular novel, Frank Yerby's *The Foxes of Harrow* (1947). Prior to his involvement with *Forever Amber*, Stahl had told Zanuck that he wanted make a film version of Paul Wellman's novel *The Walls of Jericho* saying, "I feel it is a story that has some swell characters and will make a great picture." When he directed the film version, it had originally been planned that he would be reunited with his *Leave Her to Heaven* star Gene Tierney, but she turned down the part that eventually went to Anne Baxter. Ironically, the leads were Linda Darnell (still sporting her blonde Amber tresses) and Cornel Wilde. The movie was not the success that Stahl had anticipated and he ended his career in 1949 directing the lightweight films *Father Was a Fullback* and *Oh, You Beautiful Doll.*

DAVID THURSBY
(1889-1977)

Scottish-born David Thursby was a reliable character actor who began his career in films in 1929 and appeared in over 100 motion pictures. He is also one of the few actors to appear in both versions of *Forever Amber*. In the unfinished version he is the driver of the coach which is held up by Black Jack and his gang. In the final version he is a bailiff at the court where Amber is sentenced to Newgate Prison. Although he worked for most of the major studios, he was a "regular" at Fox and appeared in such diverse films there as *Immortal Sergeant* (1943), *The Lodger* (1944), and *The Ghost and Mrs. Muir* (1947). He made his final theatrical movie in 1957, but continued to appear in television roles for nearly another decade.

PETER WHITNEY
(1916–1972)

Peter King Engle was born in New Jersey. After completing his education at the Exeter Academy in New Hampshire, he moved to California where he became an acting student at the Pasadena Community Playhouse. Changing his name to Peter Whitney, he made his film debut in *Underground* (1941), in which he played a member of the "underground" fighting for freedom in Nazi Germany. During the next few years he played supporting roles in major studio films such as *Reunion in France* (1942), *Destination Tokyo* (1943), and *Mr. Skeffington* (1944). Had it been completed, his involvement in the first version of

Peter Whitney as Black Jack Mallard.

Forever Amber would have provided him with a much more substantial part than usual and the opportunity to play a dashing, romantic character. Stills of Whitney as "Black Jack" in *Forever Amber* show him looking like a swarthy gypsy with long black hair and earrings. A studio press release at the time stated: "Black Jack Mallard…will be played on the screen by Peter Whitney who won the coveted role after 20th Century-Fox had tested 17 players, including several top stars. A tall blonde, the studio will die his hair black to match Kathleen Winsor's description of Black Jack and will give him a costly wardrobe." Peter began filming on March 30, 1946, and finished with his death scene on April 11. Although audiences never saw his performance as Black Jack, he did appear in five other films released in 1946. He continued to be a serviceable character actor, often a staple in Westerns, but also appearing in such dissimilar movies as *Day of Triumph* (1954), *The Sea Chase* (1955), *The Wonderful World of the Brothers Grimm* (1962), and *In the Heat of the Night* (1967). Between 1953 and 1972 he made continual appearances on a variety of television programs. His last film role was in *The Battle of Cable Hogue* (1970).

CORNEL WILDE
(1915-1989)

Born in New York of Hungarian immigrant parents, Cornelius Wilde had intended to become a surgeon but when he auditioned for and won a part in the 1935 Broadway play *Moon Over Mulberry Street*, he decided to pursue an acting career instead. Cornel had been a champion fencer with the U.S. Olympic team which led to his being hired as the fencing instructor for Laurence Olivier's 1940 Broadway production of *Romeo and Juliet*. He was also cast in the play in the part of "Tybalt." This exposure resulted in his being offered a contract at Warner Bros. where he appeared in small parts in three pictures (including *High Sierra*) before the studio dropped him. He was picked up by 20th Century-Fox where he continued to be cast in mostly forgettable roles until he was loaned out to Columbia on a three-picture deal. In his first film at Columbia he starred as Fredric Chopin in *A Song to Remember* (1945) and his performance garnered a Best Actor Oscar nomination. Back at Fox he was now taken more seriously and appeared in the successful film *Leave Her to Heaven* (1945). This, combined with his growing fan following, won him the male lead in *Forever Amber*. To his dismay, Cornel was one of the few cast members to be retained for the second version. He was resentful for having been "forced" into the film and refused to see it for many years. When he finally did, he was surprised that it had turned out so well and, thereafter, spoke of *Forever Amber* in glowing terms. His movie career continued for nearly four more decades during which he also produced and directed eight feature films, including the highly acclaimed *The Naked Prey* (1966), in which he also starred. His last major role was as "D'Artagnan" in *The Fifth Musketeer* (1979), although he did make a cameo appearance in *Flesh and Bullets* (1985). He died of leukemia in 1989.

Cornel Wilde as Bruce Carlton.

ORIGINAL STUDIO CASTING SUGGESTIONS

20TH CENTURY-FOX CASTING DIRECTOR WILLIAM GORDON submitted a large number of suggestions prior to the filming of the first version of *Forever Amber*. Most of the big names in Hollywood (and a lot of the smaller ones) were being considered at one time or another to play some part. Some of the suggestions are right on the mark and others are improbable, to put it mildly. According to his proposed cast listings, the only two actresses considered to play Amber were Peggy Cummins and Gene Tierney. On the list Peggy Cummins' name has been circled in red. Most of the other characters had a far greater number of names from which to choose. I have signified any comments made by William Gordon with the word "notation." Many of these casting suggestion lists were also used for the final version of *Forever Amber*.

BRUCE CARLTON

The top three choices in order were:
1. Cary Grant
2. Errol Flynn
3. Richard Greene

The other choices were:

Tyrone Power	Douglas Fairbanks
Gregory Peck	Rex Harrison
Ray Milland	David Niven
Montgomery Clift	Alan Marshal
Robert Donat	John Hodiak
Laurence Olivier	Robert Taylor
Robert Montgomery	Cornel Wilde *(circled in red)*
Dennis Morgan	

LORD ALMSBURY

Vincent Price	Reginald Gardiner
John Emery	John Sutton
Patric Knowles	Sterling Hayden
Griffith Jones	Phil Terry
George Leigh	Dennis O'Keefe
Allyn Joslyn	Lloyd Bridges
Richard Haydn	Stewart Granger
Robert Coote	Michael Rennie
Rex Harrison	Louis Hayward
John Mills	Philip Charlot
John Warburton	Richard Ney
Bramwell Fletcher	Richard Greene
George Leigh	Glenn Langan

Barry K. Barnes *(notation: Return of the Scarlet Pimpernel)*

David Niven *is also listed with an indication that he is the number one choice, but then his name is crossed out. An amended list also eliminates* Glenn Langan, Patric Knowles, Richard Ney, *and* Bramwell Fletcher.

REX MORGAN

John Sutton	Richard Ney
Dana Andrews	George Montgomery
Lee Bowman	John Payne
John Howard	Mark Stevens
Richard Greene	Glenn Langan *(circled in red)*
Cornel Wilde *(name crossed out)*	

KING CHARLES II

Reginald Gardiner *(circled in red)*
Vincent Price
Rex Harrison
Basil Rathbone
George Sanders
Claude Rains
John Gielgud
Fredric March
John Emery
Franchot Tone
Patric Knowles
Richard Ney
Kirk Douglas
Clifton Webb
Orson Welles
John Sutton
Maurice Evans
Arturo De Cordova
Melvyn Douglas
Brian Aherne
Raymond Massey
Douglas Fairbanks
Tom Helmore
Zachary Scott
Alexander Knox
Tom Conway

EARL OF RADCLYFFE

Clifton Webb *(notation: checkmark beside name)*
Leo G. Carroll
Cedric Hardwicke
Raymond Massey
Charles Laughton
Claude Rains
Monty Woolley
Basil Rathbone *(name crossed out)*
George Coulouris
Sydney Greenstreet
Robert Morley
Richard Haydn
Maurice Evans
Henry Hull

SAM DANGERFIELD

Edmund Gwenn *(notation: 1st choice)*
Dudley Digges *(notation: 2nd choice)*
Lionel Atwill
Walter Hampden
Monty Woolley
C. Aubrey Smith
Leo G. Carroll

The following actors are also listed for the part of Sam Dangerfield, but their names have been crossed out:

Charles Bickford
Reginald Gardiner
Charles Coburn
Reginald Owen
Lee Cobb
Donald Crisp
Thomas Mitchell
Dennis Hoey

NAN BRITTON

Jessica Tandy *(circled in red with notation: Film)*

Heather Angel   Queenie Leonard

June Lockhart   Maureen O'Sullivan

Eliza Sutherland *(notation: Test)*   Elsa Lanchester

The following actresses are also listed, but their names have been crossed out:

Anne Baxter   Angela Lansbury

Virginia Gilmore   Phyllis Thaxter

Betty Field   Mary Anderson

Jessica Tandy as Nan Britton.

MOTHER RED CAP

Judith Anderson
Elsa Lanchester
Flora Robson
Estelle Winwood
Isobel Elsom
Judith Evelyn *(name crossed out)*

Marjorie Rambeau
Gale Sondergaard
Agnes Moorehead
Ona Munson
Blanche Yurka
Mildred Natwick

Sara Allgood as Mother Red Cap was not one of the original casting suggestions.

BLACK JACK

John Sutton *(notation: Test)*
Victor McLaglen *(notation: Test)*
John Russell
Peter Whitney *(notation: Test)*
Barry Sullivan *(notation: No)*
Vincent Price
Dean Jagger
Robert Ryan
Albert Dekker
John Loder

Alan Napier
George Leigh
George Sanders
Victor Mature
Sonny Tufts
Steve Cochran
Henry Wilcoxon
Donald Curtis
James Craig

CORINNA

Linda Darnell
Gail Russell
Donna Reed
Evelyn Ankers
Elizabeth Ingles

Maureen O'Hara
Patricia Cameron
Patricia Roc
Susan Blanchard
Cathy Downs

Patricia Medina *(notation: Mrs. Richard Greene)*
Claire Hamilton *(notation: M. O'Hara's sister)*

MATT GOODEGROOME

Ian Wolfe *(circled in red with notation: Testing)*
Lumsden Hare
Mathew Boulton
Henry Hull

Vernon Steele
Dennis Hoey
Henry Mowbray

A later notation lists Leo G. Carroll *as first choice and* Henry Hull *as second.*

MRS. SPONG

Ethel Griffies
Sara Allgood
Margaret Wycherly
Anita Bolster
Constance Collier *(name crossed out)*

Doris Lloyd
Judith Anderson
Una O'Connor
Dodo Bernard

BARBARA PALMER
(Countess of Castlemaine)

Lynn Bari *(name crossed out)*
Geraldine Fitzgerald
Ruth Hussey
Angela Lansbury
June Duprez *(notation: See)*
Ann Richards

Patricia Morrison
Natalie Draper
Dolores Moran
Anna Lee *(notation: See)*
Jane Farrar

Natalie Draper as Barbara Palmer.

GYPSY VENDOR

Nestor Paiva   Vladimer Sokoloff
Leon Belasco *(notation: Test)*   Alex Minotis
Fritz Leiber

BOB STARLING

Ashley Cowan *(notation: Testing)*   Terry Kilburn
Roddy McDowall   Ronald Sinclaire

MRS. CLEGGAT

Eily Malyon *(circled in red)*   Kathryn Sheldon
Anita Bolster   Dodo Bernard

Eily Malyon as Mrs. Cleggat.

SEDLEY
(Sir Charles Sedley)

Reginald Denny
Paul Cavanaugh
John Warburton
Lewis Russell

Richard Haydn
Arthur Treacher
John Emery
Lester Matthews

MRS. POTERELL

Norma Varden *(circled in red with notation: Test)*
Betty Fairfax *(notation: Test)*
Edith Barrett
Margaret Hamilton

Sylvia Andrews
Eily Malyon
Dodo Bernard

Norma Varden as Mrs. Poterell.

Margo Woode as Beck Marashall.

MR. POTERELL

Lloyd Corrigan *(circled in red with notation: Test)*
Aubrey Mather *(notation: Test)*

Henry Mowbray	Pat Moriarity
Harry Allen	Billy Bevans

LITTLE BRUCE

Dean Stockwell	Gerald Perreau

MRS. CHIVERTON

Edith Barrett *(notation: 1st choice)*	Ruth Nelson
Sara Allgood	Dorothy Adams
Maureen Roden-Ryan	

BIG JOHN

John Russell *(notation: Razor's Edge test)*	Peter Whitney
Wee Willie Davis *(circled in red)*	Richard Fraser

BESS COLUMBINE

Binnie Barnes	Constance Worth
Margot Grahame	Wendy Barrie

BECK MARSHALL

Evelyn Ankers	Susan Blanchard
Mari Aldon	Binnie Barnes
Jean Wallace	Hillary Brooke
Anna Lee *(name crossed out)*	Margo Woode

DEADEYE

John Rogers *(circled in red)*	Alec Hartford
Skelton Knaggs	Clyde Cooke

TEN CAVALIERS

1. Mickey McBan	6. James Craven
2. Harry Carter	7. Sanders Clark
3. James Fuhwiler	8. John Meredith
4. Bert Hicks	9. David Cavendish
5. Brian O'Hara	10. Stanley Prager

There is also an inserted list with the heading:

PREMINGER — Tuesday, August 27, 3:30 pm

CAVALIERS — Contract Boys
1. Robert Cornel
2. Robert Ford
3. Bert Hicks
4. Fred Libby
5. Charles Lind
6. Basil Walker
7. Harry Carter

This is the only one of all the casting lists which is dated. Of this list, only Fred Libby appeared in the completed film. He played a prison ruffian who attempts to accost Amber in the Newgate Tap Room.

PROPOSED SHOOTING SCHEDULES FOR THE FIRST VERSION

March 12-13, 1946
Exterior: Marygreen
Amber buys mirror from gypsy. Bob Starling proposes.
Amber runs to house — looks off to inn. Cavaliers riding off.

March 14
Exterior: Marygreen
Amber sees Cavaliers through window.

Exterior: Golden Lion
Goodegroome sees Bruce kiss Amber, raises hell with her.

March 15
Exterior: Golden Lion
Amber rides off to London with Cavaliers.

March 16
Golden Lion Tap Room
Amber and Mrs. Poterell watch Cavaliers arrive.

March 17 — Off Sunday

March 18, 19, 20, 21
Golden Lion Tap Room
Amber takes drinks to Cavaliers.
Amber talks to Bruce — Goodegroome sees kiss.

March 22, 23
<u>Saracen's Head Inn</u>
Gumble shows rooms. Amber asks Bruce for clothes. Amber gives dinner.
Bruce has to leave.

March 24 — Off Sunday

March 25
<u>Saracen's Head Inn</u>
Amber sees Bruce and Castlemaine — Bruce tells of trip.

March 26, 27
<u>Saracen's Head Inn</u>
Bruce gone — Almsbury gives Amber money and advice.

March 28
<u>Magistrates Bench</u>
Amber committed to prison.

Peggy Cummins and Lloyd Corrigan — Golden Lion Inn.

March 29
Newgate Cell
Amber in prison — makes deal for better quarters.

March 30
Newgate Tap Room
Amber meets Black Jack — he agrees to aid her escape.

March 31 — Off Sunday

April 1, 2, 3
Newgate Tap Room

April 4
Newgate Cell
Turnkey tosses key into cell. Escape from Jail — close shots.

Peggy Cummins and Harry Wilson — Newgate Prison.

April 5
Mother Red Caps
Amber's baby is born.

April 6
Mother Red Caps
Mrs. Chiverton takes baby — plan holdup — Bess and Amber fight.

April 7 — Off Sunday

April 8, 9
Mother Red Caps
Amber sings to baby — Black Jack cleans pistol.

April 10, 11
Crossroads
Hold up — Black Jack is killed

Peggy Cummins and Peter Witney — Coach hold up.

April 12
Heath
Amber escapes from hold up.

Saracen's Head Inn
Amber arrives at Almsbury's after hold up.

April 13
Saracen's Head Inn
Almsbury sends Amber to theatre.

April 14 — Off Sunday

April 15
Saracen's Head Inn
(cont.) Almsbury sends Amber to theatre.

Theatre Royal
Beck jealous of Amber.

April 16, 17
Theatre Tiring Room
Amber and Beck argue. Amber meets Rex. Sedley gives Amber invitation.

April 18, 19
Theatre Royal
Amber plays guitar and sings — the King notices Amber.

April 20
Theatre Royal
Beck and girls throw water on Amber.

April 21 — Off Sunday

April 22
Plume of Feathers
Rex gives Amber apartment.

This was the last entry on the original proposed shooting schedule.

BIBLIOGRAPHY

Basten, Fred E. *Glorious Technicolor: The Movie's Magic Rainbow.* Cranbury, New Jersey: A.S. Barnes and Company, 1980.

Behlmer, Rudy. *Memo from Darryl F. Zanuck.* New York: Grove Press, 1993.

Cassini, Oleg. *In My Own Fashion: An Autobiography.* New York: Simon and Schuster, 1987.

Chierichetti, David. *Hollywood Costume Design.* New York: Harmony Books, 1976.

Davis, Ronald L. *Hollywood Beauty: Linda Darnell and the American Dream.* Oklahoma: University of Oklahoma Press, 1991.

Davis, Ronald L. *Oral Interview with Cornel Wilde.* August 12, 1980. Transcribed.

Dunne, Philip. *Take Two: A Life in Movies and Politics.* New York: McGraw-Hill, 1980.

Edelman, Rob, and Audrey E. Kupferberg. *Angela Lansbury: A Life on Stage and Screen.* New York: Birch Lane Press, 1996.

Falkus, Christopher. *The Life and Times of Charles II.* New York: Doubleday and Company, 1972.

Flamini, Roland. *Scarlett, Rhett, and a Cast of Thousands.* New York: Macmillan Publishing Company, 1975.

Fraser, George MacDonald. *The Hollywood History of the World.* New York: Beech Tree Books, 1988.

Gale, Thomson. *Contemporary Authors: Biography- Kathleen Winsor.* Amazon. Digital Document.

Gussow, Mel. *Don't Say Yes Until I Finish Talking: A Biography of Darryl F. Zanuck.* New York: Doubleday and Company, 1971.

Hanson, Patricia King (Executive Editor). *American Film Institute Catalog 1941-1950.* Berkeley University of California Press, 1999.

Higham, Charles. *Hollywood Cameraman: Sources of Light.* Bloomington: Indiana University Press, 1970.

Kim, Jennifer. *20th Century American Bestsellers.* Graduate School of Library and Information Science. Digital Document.

Lamparski, Richard. *Whatever Became Of? 10th Series.* New York: Crown Publishers, 1986.

Latham, Harold S. *My Life in Publishing.* New York; Dutton, 1966.

Manhattan, Avro. *The Vatican in World Politics.* Gaer Associations, 1949.

Miller, Frank. *Censored Hollywood*. Atlanta, Georgia: Turner Publishing, 1994.

Moore, Dr. Nichole. *Secrets of the Censors: Obscenity in the Archives*. National Archives of Australia, May 2, 2005.

Moreno, Eduardo. *The Films of Susan Hayward*. New Jersey; Citadel Press, 1979.

Nugent, Frank S. "Forever Amber or Crime Doesn't Pay," *The New Yorker Magazine*, August 4, 1946, pp. 12-13.

Persico, Joseph E. *Roosevelt's Secret War*. New York: Random House, 2001.

Pratley, Gerald. *The Cinema of Otto Preminger*. New York: Castle Books, 1971.

Preminger, Otto. *Preminger: An Autobiography*. New York: Doubleday and Company, 1977.

Rechy, John. "A Spirit Preserved in Amber," *Los Angeles Times Book Review*, June 15, 2003,

Shepherd, D. William (Editor). *Planes of the 449th Bomb Group in WWII*. Panama City, Fl: Norfield Publishing.

Solomon, Aubrey. *Twentieth Century-Fox: A Corporate and Financial History*. Metuchen, New Jersey: Scarecrow Press, 1988.

Tierney, Gene (with Mickey Herskowitz). *Self-Portrait*. Wyden Books, 1978.

Vanderbeets, Richard. *George Sanders: An Exhausted Life*. New York: Madison Books, 1990.

Williams. Lucy Chase. *The Complete Films of Vincent Price*. New York: Citadel Press, 1995.

Winsor, Kathleen. *Forever Amber*. New York: Macmillan Company, 1944.

Winsor, Kathleen. *Star Money*. New York: Appleton-Century-Crofts, 1950.

INDEX

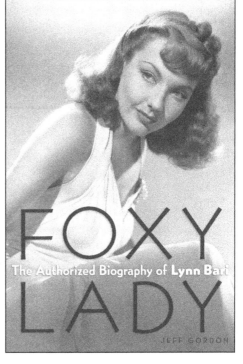
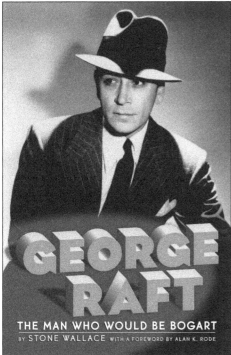

CPSIA information can be obtained
at www.ICGtesting.com
Printed in the USA
LVHW080315270421
685690LV00023B/364